Street by Street

ALDERSHO
CAMBERLE M

FARNBOROUGH, FLEET

Ash, Bagshot, Bentley, Bisley, Blackwater, Brookwood, Cove, Crowthorne, Frimley, Knaphill, Lightwater, Rowledge, Sandhurst, Windlesham, Yateley

3rd edition August 2008

Original edition printed September 2002

Published by AA Publishing (a trading name of Automobile Association Developments Limited, whose registered office is Fanum House, Basing View, Basingstoke, Hampshire RG21 4EA. Registered number 1878835).

Produced by the Mapping Services Department of The Automobile Association. (A03663)

A CIP Catalogue record for this book is available from the British Library.

Printed by Oriental Press in Dubai

 The publishers would welcome information to correct any errors or omissions and to keep this atlas up to date. Please write to Publishing, The Automobile Association, Fanum House (FH12), Basing View, Basingstoke, Hampshire, RG21 4EA. E-mail: *streetbystreet@theaa.com*

Ref: ML164y

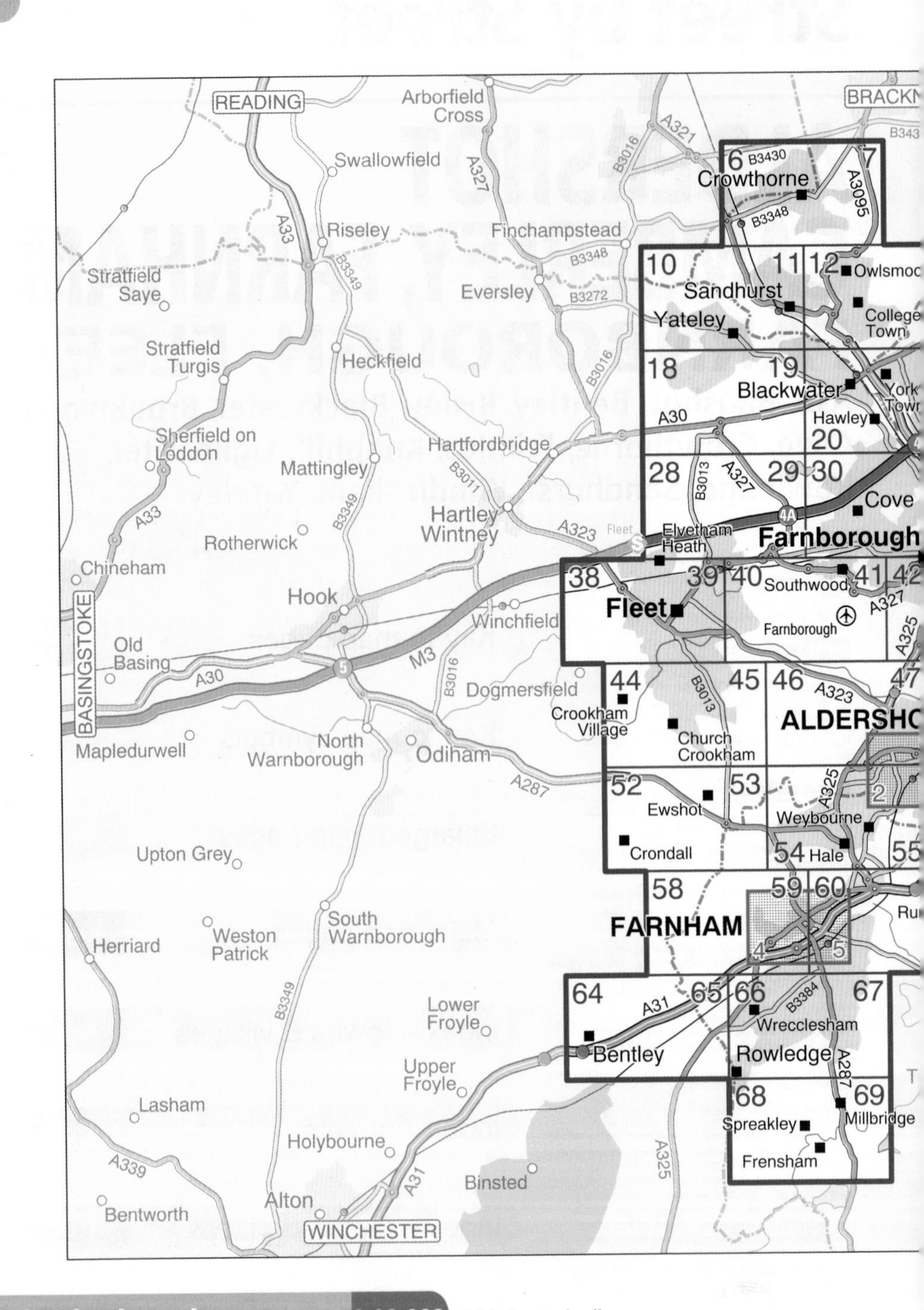

Scale of enlarged map pages 1:10,000 6.3 inches to 1 mile

National Grid references are shown on the map frame of each page.
Red figures denote the 100 km square and blue figures the 1 km square.
Example, page 7: Broadmoor Hospital 485 164

The reference can also be written using the National Grid two-letter prefix shown on this page, where 4 and 1 are replaced by SU to give SU8564.

4.2 inches to 1 mile **Scale of main map pages** **1:15,000**

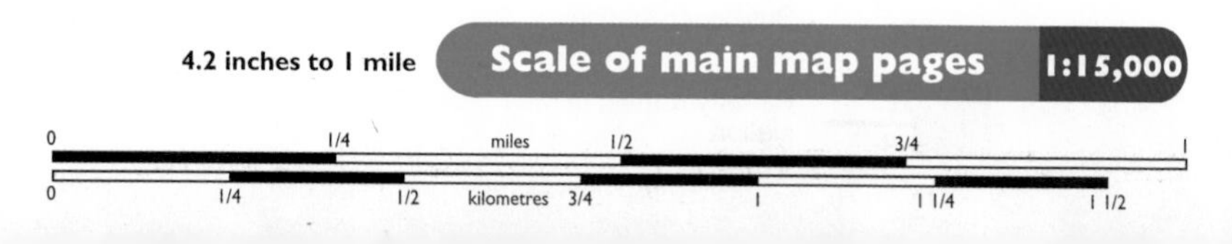

Junction 9

Motorway & junction

Services

Motorway service area

Primary road single/dual carriageway

Services

Primary road service area

A road single/dual carriageway

B road single/dual carriageway

Other road single/dual carriageway

Minor/private road, access may be restricted

One-way street

Pedestrian area

Track or footpath

Road under construction

Road tunnel

30

Speed camera site (fixed location) with speed limit in mph

V

Speed camera site (fixed location) with variable speed limit

40

Section of road with two or more fixed camera sites; speed limit in mph or variable

50 50

Average speed (SPECS™) camera system with speed limit in mph

P

Parking

P+

Park & Ride

Bus/coach station

Railway & main railway station

Railway & minor railway station

Underground station

Light railway & station

Preserved private railway

LC

Level crossing

Tramway

Ferry route

Airport runway

County, administrative boundary

Mounds

17

Page continuation 1:15,000

3

Page continuation to enlarged scale 1:10,000

River/canal, lake, pier

Aqueduct, lock, weir

465

Winter Hill

Peak (with height in metres)

Beach

Woodland

Park

Cemetery

Built-up area

	Industrial/business building
	Leisure building
	Retail building
	Other building
	City wall
A&E	Hospital with 24-hour A&E department
PO	Post Office
	Public library
i	Tourist Information Centre
i	Seasonal Tourist Information Centre
	Petrol station, 24 hour Major suppliers only
	Church/chapel
	Public toilet, with facilities for the less able
PH	Public house AA recommended
	Restaurant AA inspected
Madeira Hotel	Hotel AA inspected
	Theatre or performing arts centre
	Cinema
	Golf course
	Camping AA inspected
	Caravan site AA inspected
	Camping & caravan site AA inspected
	Theme park
	Abbey, cathedral or priory
	Castle
	Historic house or building
Wakehurst Place NT	National Trust property
M	Museum or art gallery
	Roman antiquity
	Ancient site, battlefield or monument
	Industrial interest
	Garden
	Garden Centre Garden Centre Association Member
	Garden Centre Wyevale Garden Centre
	Arboretum
	Farm or animal centre
	Zoological or wildlife collection
	Bird collection
	Nature reserve
	Aquarium
V	Visitor or heritage centre
	Country park
	Cave
	Windmill
	Distillery, brewery or vineyard
•	Other place of interest

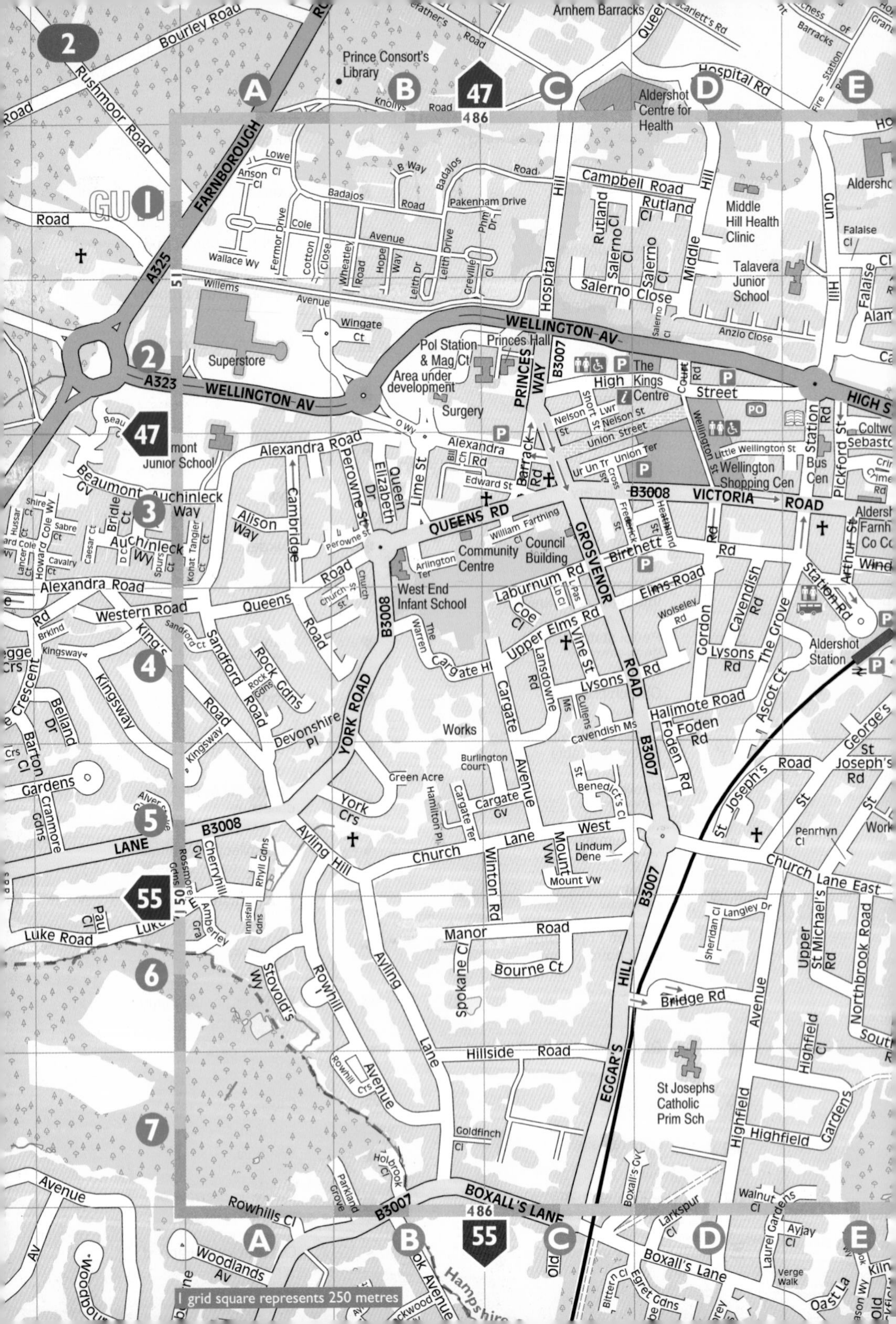
2
A
B
C
D
E
47
486
55
1
2
3
4
5
6
7
Bourley Road
Rushmoor Road
FARNBOROUGH
A325
Prince Consort's Library
Knollys Road
Arnhem Barracks
Queen
Scarlett's Rd
Barracks
Fire Station
Hospital Rd
Aldershot Centre for Health
Lowe Cl
Anson Cl
B Way
Badajos Road
Pakenham Drive
Campbell Road
Rutland
Rutland Cl
Middle Hill Health Clinic
Fermor Drive
Cole
Avenue
Wallace Wy
Cotton
Close
Wheatley
Road
Hope
Way
Leith Dr
Leith Drive
Greville Cl
Hospital Hill
Salerno Cl
Salerno Close
Middle Hill
Talavera Junior School
Falaise Cl
Gun Hill
Aldershot
Willems Avenue
Wingate Ct
Superstore
WELLINGTON AV
A323
Pol Station & Mag Ct
Princes Hall
Area under development
Surgery
PRINCES WAY
B3007
The Kings Centre
High Street
Court Rd
HIGH ST
Anzio Close
Beaumont Junior School
Alexandra Road
Cambridge
Perowne St
Elizabeth Dr
Queen
Lime St
Alexandra Rd
Edward St
Barrack Rd
Nelson Lwr
Short St
Nelson St
Union Street
Union Ter
Cross St
Wellington St
Little Wellington St
Wellington Shopping Cen
Station Rd
Bus Cen
Pickford St
Coltwo
Sebasto
Beaumont Gv
Auchinleck Way
Auchinleck Wy
Shire Ct
Hussar Ct
Cole Ct
Howard Cole Wy
Sabre Ct
Bridle Ct
Caesar Ct
Lancer Ct
Cavalry Ct
Spurs Ct
Kohat Tangier Ct
Alison Way
QUEENS RD
William Farthing Cl
Community Centre
Council Building
Arlington Ter
West End Infant School
GROSVENOR ROAD
B3008
VICTORIA ROAD
Frederick St
Heathland St
Birchett Rd
Gordon Rd
Aldershot Farnh Co C
Arthur St
Station Rd
Laburnum Rd
Lb Cl
L Pas
Elms Road
Wolseley Rd
Cavendish Rd
The Grove
Coe Cl
Upper Elms Rd
Vine St
Alexandra Road
Western Road
Queens Road
Church St
Church
Sandford Ct
Sandford Road
Rock Gdns
Kingsway
King's
Crescent
Belland Dr
Barton Cl
Gardens
Cranmore Gdns
Road
Devonshire Pl
YORK ROAD
B3008
The Warren
Cargate Hl
Lansdowne Rd
Cargate Avenue
Lysons Rd
Cullens Ms
Cavendish Ms
Halimote Road
Foden Rd
Lysons Rd
Ascot Ct
Aldershot Station
Works
Burlington Court
Green Acre
York Crs
Hamilton Pl
Cargate Ter
Cargate Gv
St Benedict's Cl
West Lane
Lindum Dene
Mount Vw
St Joseph's Road
George's
St Joseph's Rd
Penrhyn Cl
Church Lane East
LANE
B3008
Cherryhill Gv
Rossmore Gdns
Rhyll Gdns
Ayling Hill
Church Lane
Winton Rd
Amberley
Innisfail Gdns
Paul Cl
Luke Road
Manor Road
Spokane Cl
Bourne Ct
Sheridan Cl
Langley Dr
Upper St Michael's Rd
Northbrook Road
Stovold's Wy
Rowhill
Ayling Lane
EGGAR'S HILL
B3007
Bridge Rd
Avenue
Highfield Cl
South
Hillside Road
St Josephs Catholic Prim Sch
Rowhill Crs
Avenue
Highfield Gardens
Highfield
Goldfinch Cl
Holbrook Cl
Parkland Grove
Boxall's Gv
Walnut Cl
BOXALL'S LANE
B3007
Rowhills Cl
Avenue
Woodlands Av
Larkspur Cl
Laurel Gardens
Ayjay Cl
Verge Walk
Boxall's Lane
Bittern Cl
Egret Gdns
Old
Oast La
Kiln
1 grid square represents 250 metres
Hampshire

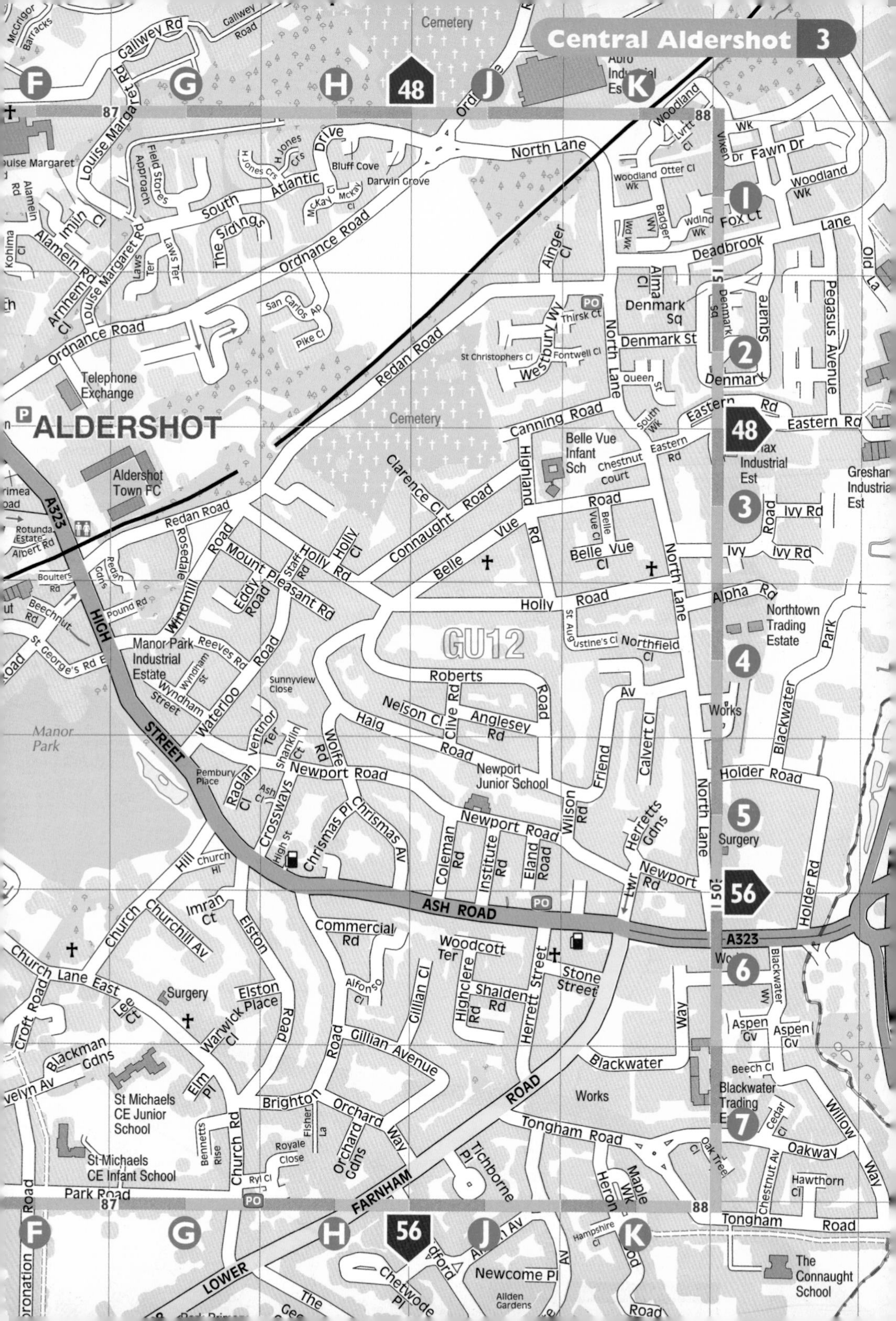
Cemetery
48
F
G
H
J
K
87
88
Galliwey Rd
Gallwey Road
McGrigor Barracks
Louise Margaret Rd
Field Stores Approach
H Jones Crs
Atlantic Drive
Bluff Cove
Darwin Grove
McKay Cl
South
The Sidings
Ordnance Road
North Lane
Alamein Rd
Imjin Cl
Arnhem Cl
Laws Ter
San Carlos Ap
Pike Cl
Telephone Exchange
ALDERSHOT
Aldershot Town FC
Redan Road
A323
Rotunda Estate
Albert Rd
Boulters Rd
Beechnut Rd
St George's Rd
HIGH STREET
Manor Park Industrial Estate
Manor Park
Wyndham Street
Reeves Rd
Rosedale
Windmill Road
Eddy Road
Mount Pleasant Rd
Staff Rd
Holly Rd
Holly Cl
Connaught Road
Clarence Cl
Canning Road
Highland Rd
Belle Vue Infant Sch
Chestnut Court
Belle Vue Road
Belle Vue Cl
Holly Road
St Augustine's Cl
Northfield Cl
GU12
Roberts Road
Nelson Cl
Clive Rd
Anglesey Rd
Haig Road
Wolfe Rd
Waterloo Road
Ventnor Ter
Shanklin Ct
Sunnyview Close
Newport Road
Newport Junior School
Pembury Place
Raglan Cl
Ash Cl
Crossways
Chrismas Pl
Chrismas Av
Coleman Rd
Institute Rd
Eland Road
Wilson Rd
Friend Av
Calvert Cl
Herretts Gdns
Lwr Newport Rd
ASH ROAD
PO
Church Hill
Church Hl
Imran Ct
Churchill Av
Elston Road
Commercial Rd
Woodcott Ter
Herrett Street
Stone Street
Alfonso Cl
Gillian Cl
Gillian Avenue
Highclere Rd
Shalden Rd
Church Lane East
Croft Road
Lee Ct
Surgery
Elston Place
Warwick Cl
Blackman Gdns
Evelyn Av
St Michaels CE Junior School
St Michaels CE Infant School
Elm Pl
Bennetts Rise
Church Rd
Brighton Road
Fisher La
Orchard Way
Orchard Gdns
Royale Close
Ryl Cl
Park Road
Coronation Road
LOWER FARNHAM ROAD
56
Tichborne Pl
Chetwode Pl
Newcome Pl
Allden Gardens
Hampshire Cl
Heron Wk
Maple Wk
Tongham Road
Blackwater Way
Works
Westbury Wy
Thirsk Ct
Fontwell Cl
St Christophers Cl
Ainger Cl
Alma Cl
Denmark Sq
Denmark St
Denmark Square
Queen St
South Wk
Eastern Rd
Woodland Wk
Otter Cl
Badger Wy
Wdlnd Wk
Fox Ct
Deadbrook Lane
Vixen Dr
Fawn Dr
Pegasus Avenue
Old La
Lyrtt
Eastern Rd
Industrial Est
Gresham Industrial Est
Ivy Road
Ivy Rd
Alpha Rd
Northtown Trading Estate
Park
Blackwater
Holder Road
Holder Rd
Surgery
Aspen Gv
Beech Cl
Blackwater Trading Est
Cedar Cl
Oak Tree Cl
Chestnut Av
Oakway
Hawthorn Cl
Willow Way
Tongham Road
The Connaught School
1
2
3
4
5
6
7

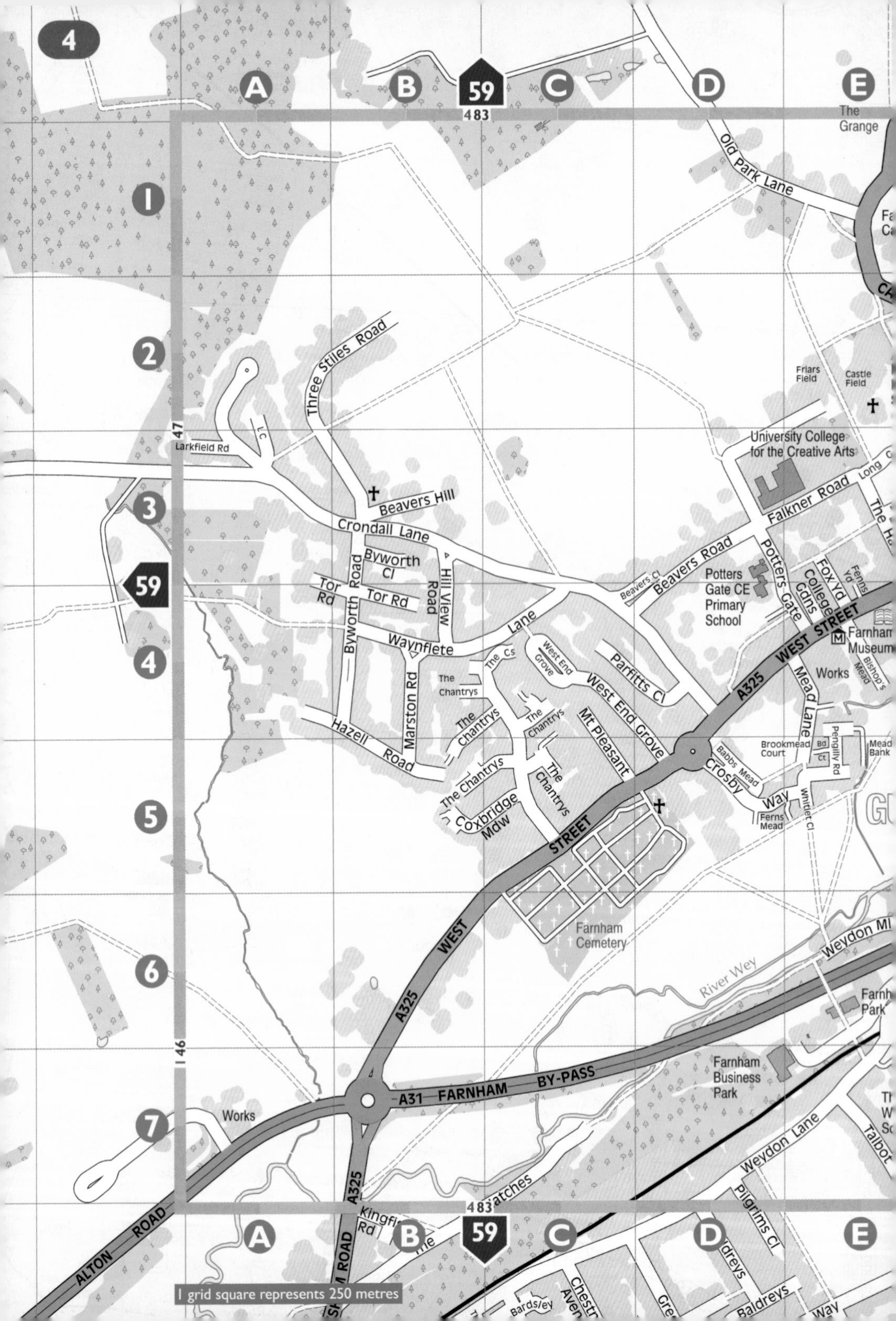

59
483
The Grange
Old Park Lane
Three Stiles Road
Larkfield Rd
Ct
Beavers Hill
Crondall Lane
Byworth Cl
Byworth Road
Tor Rd
Tor Rd
Hill View Road
Waynflete Lane
Marston Rd
Hazell Road
The Cs
The Chantrys
The Chantrys
The Chantrys
The Chantrys
The Chantrys
The Chantrys
Coxbridge Mdw
West End Grove
West End Grove
Mt Pleasant
Parfitts Cl
Beavers Cl
Beavers Road
Potters Gate CE Primary School
Potters Gate
College Gdns
Fox Yd
Fenns Yd
Friars Field
Castle Field
University College for the Creative Arts
Falkner Road
Long
A325 WEST STREET
Farnham Museum
Bishop's Mead
Works
Mead Lane
Brookmead Court
Bd
Ct
Pengilly Rd
Mead Bank
Babbs Mead
Crosby Way
Ferns Mead
Whitlet Cl
STREET
A325 WEST
Farnham Cemetery
River Wey
Weydon Mi
Farnham Park
Farnham Business Park
A31 FARNHAM BY-PASS
Works
Weydon Lane
Talbot
Pilgrims Cl
ALTON ROAD
A325
Kingfi
Rd
The
Baldreys
Bardsley
Way
1 46
47
1 grid square represents 250 metres

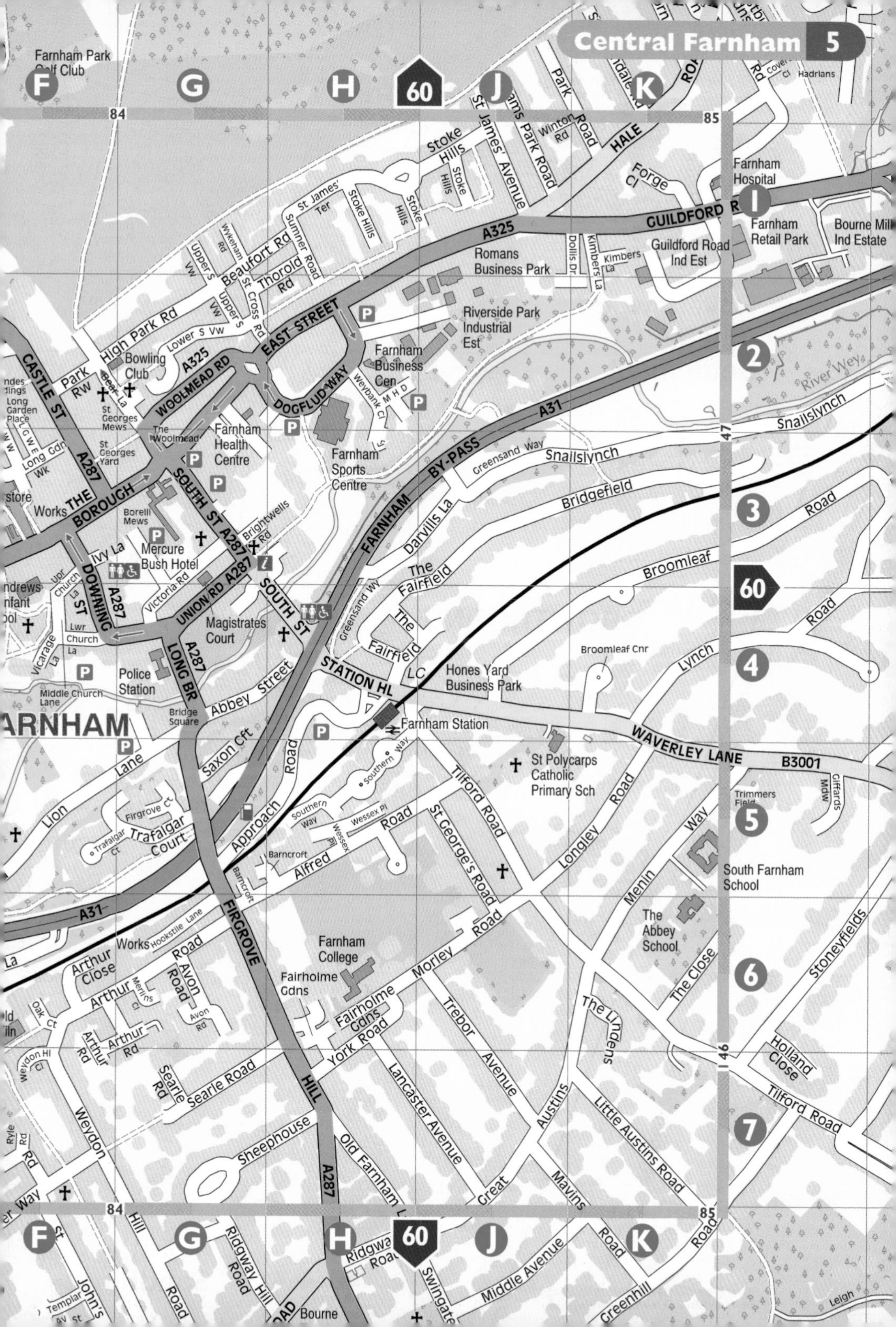

Farnham Park Golf Club
F
G
H
60
J
K
84
85
Park Road
Winton Rd
HALE
St James' Avenue
St James Park Road
Stoke Hills
Forge Cl
Farnham Hospital
GUILDFORD RD
A325
Farnham Retail Park
Bourne Mill Ind Estate
Guildford Road Ind Est
Romans Business Park
Dollis Dr
Kimbers La
St James' Ter
Sumner Road
Stoke Hills
Beaufort Rd
Thorold Rd
St Cross Rd
Upper S Vw
Wykeham Rd
EAST STREET
Riverside Park Industrial Est
High Park Rd
Lower S Vw
Park Rw
Bear La
Bowling Club
A325
WOOLMEAD RD
DOGFLUD WAY
Farnham Business Cen
Weybank Cl
M H D
River Wey
2
Snailslynch
A31
CASTLE ST
Long Garden Place
Long Gdn Wk
St Georges Mews
St Georges Yard
The Woolmead
Farnham Health Centre
Farnham Sports Centre
FARNHAM BY-PASS
Greensand Way
Snailslynch
47
A287
THE BOROUGH
SOUTH ST A287
Works
Borelli Mews
Brightwells Rd
Darvills La
Bridgefield
3
Road
Ivy La
Mercure Bush Hotel
Victoria Rd
UNION RD A287
The Fairfield
Broomleaf
60
Upr Church La
DOWNING ST
A287
Lwr Church La
Vicarage La
Magistrates Court
SOUTH ST
Greensand Wy
The Fairfield
Road
Broomleaf Cnr
Lynch
4
Police Station
Middle Church Lane
LONG BR
A287
STATION HL
LC
Hones Yard Business Park
Abbey Street
Bridge Square
FARNHAM
Farnham Station
WAVERLEY LANE
B3001
Saxon Cft
Road
Southern Way
St Polycarps Catholic Primary Sch
Lion Lane
Firgrove Ct
Trafalgar Court
Trafalgar Ct
Approach
Southern Way
Wessex Pl
Road
St George's Road
Tilford Road
Longley Road
Way
Trimmers Field
Giffards Mdw
5
Barncroft
Alfred
Menin
South Farnham School
A31
FIRGROVE
Hookstile Lane
Works
Arthur Close
Road
Avon Road
Farnham College
Morley Road
The Abbey School
The Close
Stoneyfields
6
Oak Ct
Arthur
Merlins Cl
Avon Rd
Fairholme Gdns
Fairholme Gdns
York Road
Trebor Avenue
The Lindens
Holland Close
Arthur Rd
Arthur Rd
Weydon Hl Cl
Searle Rd
Searle Road
HILL
Lancaster Avenue
Austins
Little Austins Road
46
Tilford Road
7
Weydon
Ryle Rd
Sheephouse
Old Farnham La
A287
Great
Mavins
Way
84
85
F
G
H
60
J
K
Hill
Ridgway Road
Ridgway Road
Swingate
Middle Avenue
Road
Road
Road
John's
Templar
Ridgway Hill
ROAD
Bourne
Greenhill
Leigh

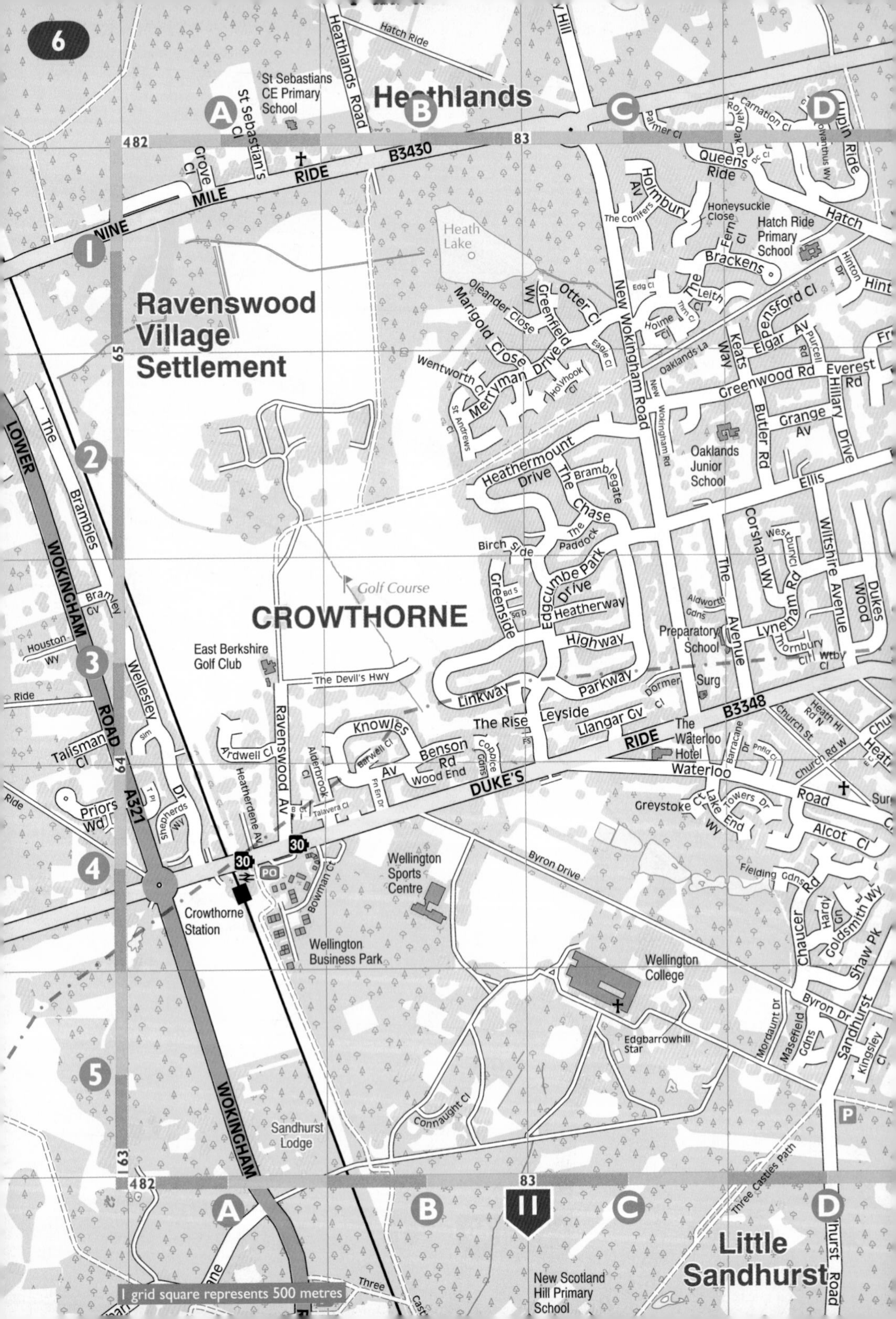

Heathlands
Ravenswood Village Settlement
CROWTHORNE
Little Sandhurst
St Sebastians CE Primary School
Hatch Ride Primary School
Oaklands Junior School
Preparatory School
East Berkshire Golf Club
Golf Course
Heath Lake
The Waterloo Hotel
Wellington Sports Centre
Wellington Business Park
Wellington College
Crowthorne Station
Sandhurst Lodge
Edgbarrowhill Star
New Scotland Hill Primary School
Nine Mile Ride
B3430
B3348
Duke's Ride
Waterloo Road
Lower Wokingham Road
A321
Wokingham Road
New Wokingham Road
Heathlands Road
Hatch Ride
Ravenswood Av
Heatherdene Av
Byron Drive
Three Castles Path
Sandhurst Road
The Devil's Hwy
Linkway
Parkway
Highway
Heatherway
Edgcumbe Park Drive
Greenside
Birch Side
The Paddock
The Chase
Bramblegate
Heathermount Drive
Merryman Drive
Marigold Close
Oleander Close
Greenfield Wy
Otter Cl
Wentworth Cl
St Andrews Cl
Holmbury Av
The Conifers
Queens Ride
Honeysuckle Close
Brackens
The Leith
Holme Cl
Fern Cl
Pensford Cl
Elgar Av
Keats Way
Oaklands La
Greenwood Rd
Everest Rd
Hillary Drive
Grange Av
Butler Rd
Ellis
Corsham Wy
Westbury Cl
Lyneham Rd
Wiltshire Avenue
Dukes Wood
Thornbury Cl
The Avenue
Aldworth Gdns
Dormer Cl
Llangar Gv
Leyside
The Rise
Coppice Gdns
Benson Rd
Wood End
Knowles Av
Barwell Cl
Alderbrook Cl
Ardwell Cl
Talavera Cl
Bowman Ct
Greystoke Ct
Lake End Wy
Towers Dr
Barracane Dr
Church St
Church Rd W
Heath Hl Rd N
Alcot Cl
Fielding Gdns
Chaucer Rd
Hardy Gn
Goldsmith Wy
Shaw Pk
Byron Dr
Mordaunt Dr
Masefield Gdns
Kingsley Cl
Connaught Cl
The Brambles
Bramley Gv
Houston Wy
Wellesley Dr
Talisman Cl
Priors Wd
Shepherds Wy
Grove Cl
St Sebastian's Cl
Palmer Cl
Carnation Cl
Royal Oak Dr
Lupin Ride
Hinton Dr
Purcell Rd
New Wokingham Rd
Surg
PO
482
83
65
64
63
A B C D
1 2 3 4 5
11
30
1 grid square represents 500 metres

B3430
FORESTERS
A3095
Bracknell Rd
Telford Av
Brunel Dr
Lanchester Drive
Crowthorne Business Centre
Mcdm Av
Old
Wokingham Road
Maple Drive
Drive
Old Sawmill La
Lyon Road
Celandine Cl
Dwdng Ct
Brookers Row
BRACKNELL ROAD
B3348
ROAD
A3095
FORESTERS WAY
RG45
Circle Hill Road
Avenue
New Rd
PO
BRACKNELL
Brookers Cnr
Upr Broadmoor Rd
White City
Upper Broadmoor Rd
Club La
Kentigern Drive
The Ter
Street
Forest Rd
Napier Road
Napier Cl
Cricket Fld Gv
Broadmoor Hospital
Cambridge Road
Wellington Road
Furze Hl Crs
Mulberry Cl
Chaplain's Hill
School Hill
Lower Broadmoor Road
Lower Broadmoor Road
Eastern Lane
Three Castles Path
Three Castles
Broadmoor Farm
FORESTERS WAY
Poppy
Amblsd
Grant Rd
Addiscombe Rd
Gordon Rd
Broadmoor CP School
Road
Jerome Cnr
South Meadow
South Road
Sports Centre
Woods
85
86
65
64
63
E
F
G
H
1
2
3
4
5
12
A3095
RACKSTRAW
Hexham Cl
Way
Dovedale Cl
Copperfield Av
Magdalene R
Merton Cl

Golf Course
A
B
C
D
490
91
1
2
3
4
5
65
64
63
Bracknell Forest
Surrey County
A322
BRACKNELL ROAD
Dukes Covert
Dukes Hl
HALLGROVE
Hall Grove
Rapley Lake
Premier Inn
Bagshot Park
A322
GROVE END
Windlesham Golf Club
Bagshot Station
Lory Ridge
Anderson Pl
Golf Course
Station Rd
BRIDGE RD
Hart Dene Ct
Talbot Pl
Gloucester Road
Faulkner Pl
Hewlett Pl
Kepple Pl
Freemantle Rd
Bell Pl
Duval Pl
A322
BAGSHOT
Surgery
Park View
Park St
High St
HIGH ST
GUILDFORD RD
Wardle Cl
The Sq
PO
Waverley Rd
Cedar Cl
St Marys Gdn
Bagshot Green
Heath Rd
Manor Way
NEW RD
Swift La
Swift
Vicarage Road
Church Road
Mill Cl
St Annes Gld
Mill Fld
College Ride
Connaught Rd
Wellesley Cl
Ride
Heywood Dr
Higgs La
Higgs Lane
Pinewood Gdns
Bagshot School
A30
15
College
Yaverland Dr
Lambourne Dr
Chapel Lane
Chapel La
Brook Rd
Green Lane
Broomsquires Rd
Elizabeth Av
Guildford
Stable Croft
Pennyhill Park Hotel
1 grid square represents 500 metres
Connaught County Junior School
Butler Rd
Rd
LONDON ROAD

Country Gardens Estate
Wyevale Garden Centre
Windlesham Hall
A30 LONDON ROAD
SUNNINGHILL RD
Erl Wood Manor
PH
Snows Paddock
Bosman Dr
Windlesham Court
Chewter La
Newark Road
Windlesham
Ride
Court
Poplar Avenue
Rosslea
Turpins Rise
Newark Rd
Hawkes Leap
Leycester Cl
Highwayman's Rdg
Mill Pond Rd
Fosters Gv
Snows
SCHOOL ROAD
GU20
Windlesham Village Infant School
Wynsham Wy
White Hl
Moor Pl
Woodcote House School
Hatton Hill
Westwood Road
Westwood Road
B386
KENNEL LANE
Cochrane Pl
Govett Gv
Owen Rd
Kent Rd
Caldwell Rd
Kings Lane
Ramsay Rd
CHERTSEY RO
Finney Dr
Cooper Rd
Baigents La
Atfield Grove
School La
Cricketers La
Windle Close
WINDLESHAM
UPDOWN HILL
Edward Road
Oakwood Road
Birch Rd
Heathpark Drive
Pound Lane
Church Road
New Road
Birch Hall
Graham Rd
Windmill Field
Updown Hl
Pine Grove
Rectory Lane
Hatch End
Thorndown Lane
Broadley Green
Hutton Cl
Orchard Hl
Scutley La
Old House Lane
Ashleigh Farm
Works
M3
93
94
65
64
63
E
F
G
H
1
2
3
4
5
16
Broadway Road

Lower Sandhurst Road
Hall Farm
Moor Green Farm
Blackwater River
Wokingham
Hampshire County
Three Castles Path
Mill Farm
Eversley CC
Eversley Cross
Hall's Way
Fox Lane
Millbridge Rd
Blaire Pk
River Rd
Coombe Rd
Canberra Close
Mayflower Dr
Moulsham Lane
Ives Cl
Crosby Gdns
EVERSLEY RD
EVERSLEY ROAD
READING ROAD
B3272
Vicarage Road
Crondall End
Chandlers Lane
Vicarage Lane
Broome Cl
W Fryerne
The Gallop
Croft Lane
Firglen Drive
Bridge Wk
Church Vw
Village Way
White Lion Wy
Brooklands
Celandine Ct
Fallowfield
Castor Ct
West Green
Frensham Cl
The Link
Yateley Green
Clover La
Bracken La
Ilex Cl
Robins Gv Crs
Firgrove Road
Bramling Av
Aylesham Way
Partridge Av
Swallow Cl
Blakes Ride
Selwyn Dr
Colwyn Cl
Connaught Cl
School Lane
Lwr Canes
Surgery
Rokes Pl
Tesimond Dr
Monteagle La
Old School La
Macrae Rd
Hall Lane
Willowford
Health Centre
Lawford Crescent
Cranford Park Drive
Calcott Pk
Home Park Rd
Parkfields
Yateley Infant Sch
GU46
Manor
Ryves Av
Tresham Crs
Westfield Infant School
Westfield Junior School
Yateley School
Wistaria La
The Dell
Lymington Av
Farm View
Hall Farm Crescent
Oldcorne Hollow
Hilltop Vw
Byways
YA
480
81
63
62
61
18
1 grid square represents 500 metres

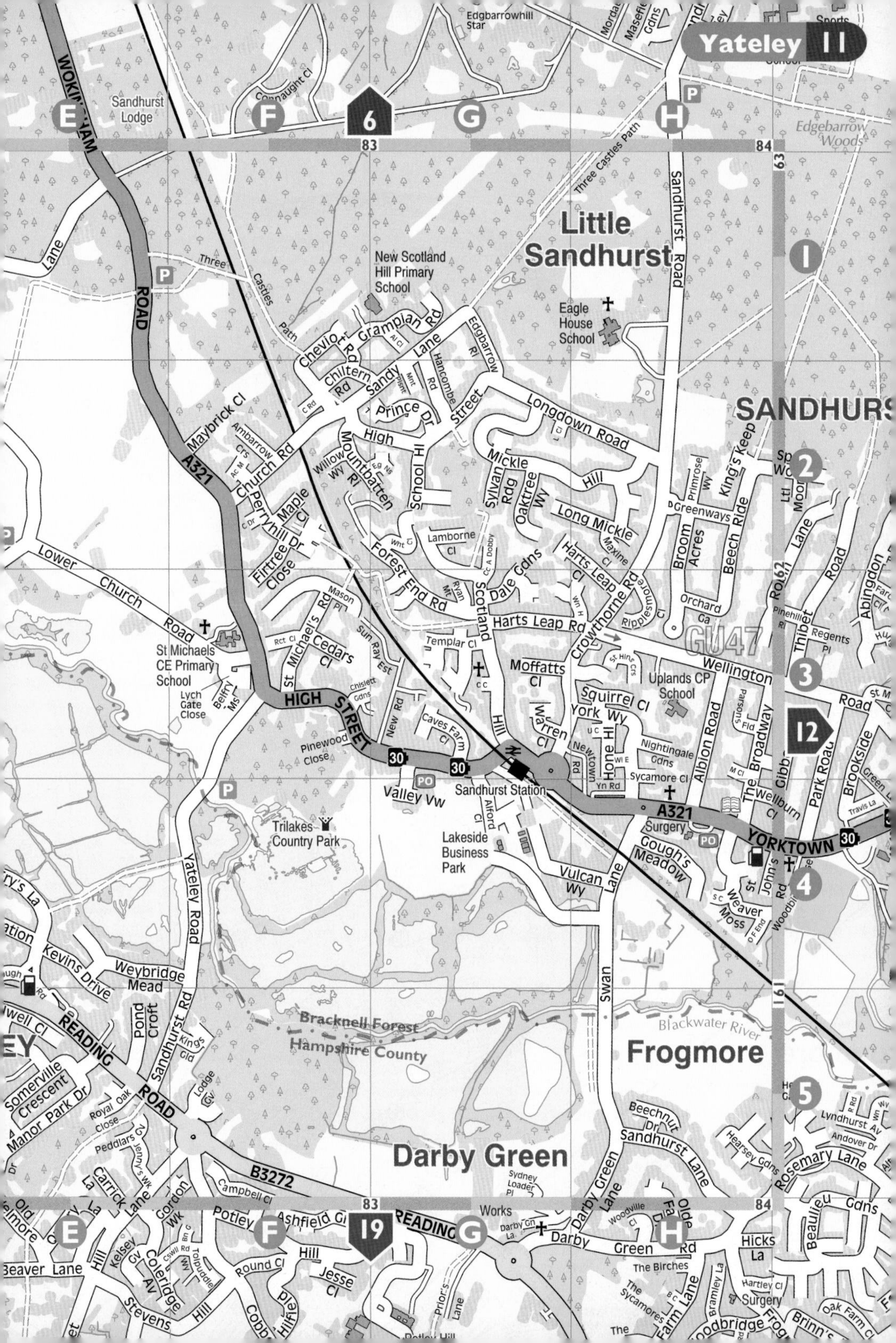
Little Sandhurst
SANDHURS
Frogmore
Darby Green
Edgbarrowhill Star
Sandhurst Lodge
Edgebarrow Woods
Connaught Cl
Three Castles Path
Sandhurst Road
New Scotland Hill Primary School
Eagle House School
WOKINGHAM ROAD
A321
Lane
Three Castles Path
Cheviot Rd
Grampian Rd
Chiltern Rd
Sandy Lane
Hancombe Rd
Edgbarrow Ri
Prince Dr
High Street
Longdown Road
Maybrick Cl
Ambarrow Crs
Church Rd
Mountbatten Ri
Willow Wy
School Hl
Mickle Hill
Sylvan Rdg
Oaktree Wy
Long Mickle
Maxine Cl
Primrose Wy
King's Keep
Greenways
Broom Acres
Beech Ride
Perryhill Dr
Maple Cl
Firtree Close
Lamborne Cl
Forest End Rd
Dale Gdns
Harts Leap Cl
Harts Leap Rd
Crowthorne Rd
Ripplesmore Cl
Orchard Ga
Lower Church Road
Mason Pl
St Michael's Rd
Cedars Cl
Sun Ray Est
Templar Cl
Scotland Hill
Moffatts Cl
Warren Cl
Squirrel Cl
York Wy
Uplands CP School
Albion Road
Wellington Road
The Broadway
St Michaels CE Primary School
Lych Gate Close
Belfry Ms
HIGH STREET
Chislett Gdns
New Rd
Caves Farm Cl
Pinewood Close
Valley Vw
Sandhurst Station
Alford Cl
Newtown Rd
Hone Hl
Nightingale Cdns
Sycamore Cl
Yn Rd
The Wellburn Cl
Park Road
Brookside
Gibbs
Thibet Road
Regents Pl
Pinehill Rd
Abingdon
Lane
Ltl Moor
Travis La
Trilakes Country Park
Lakeside Business Park
Vulcan Wy
Swan Lane
Gough's Meadow
Surgery
YORKTOWN
St John's Rd
Weaver Moss
Yateley Road
Kevins Drive
Weybridge Mead
Pond Croft
Sandhurst Rd
Kings Cld
Lodge Gv
READING ROAD
Somerville Crescent
Manor Park Dr
Royal Oak Close
Peddlars Gv
Jenny's Wk
Bracknell Forest
Hampshire County
Blackwater River
Beechnut Dr
Sandhurst Lane
Hearsey Gdns
Rosemary Lane
Lyndhurst Av
Andover Dr
B3272
Campbell Cl
Sydney Loader Pl
Darby Green Lane
Carrick Lane
Gordon Wk
Potley Hill
Ashfield Gn
Works
READING
Darby Gn La
Darby Green Rd
Woodville Cl
Olde Farm Dr
Hicks La
Beaulieu Gdns
Kelsey Gv
Coleridge Av
Tolpuddle Wy
Round Cl
Hill
Jesse Cl
Beaver Lane
Stevens Hill
Prior's Lane
The Birches
The Sycamores
Farm Lane
Bramley La
Hartley Cl
Surgery
Oak Farm Cl
GU47
Sports
School
6
12
19
30
83
84
63
62
61
E
F
G
H
I
2
3
4
5

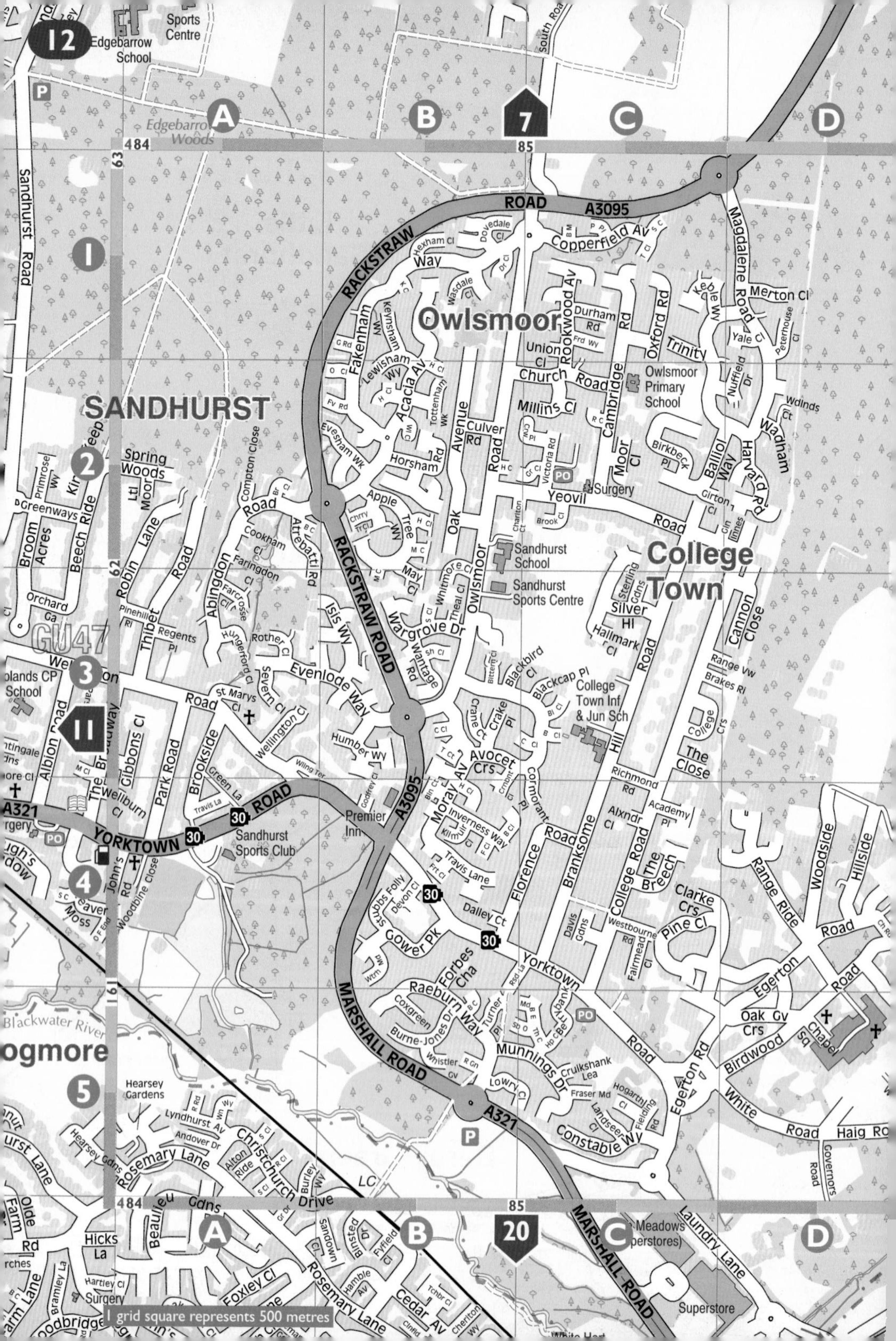

12
Edgebarrow School
Sports Centre
Edgebarrow Woods
South Road
7
A
B
C
D
484
85
63
62
61
1
2
3
4
5
Sandhurst Road
RACKSTRAW ROAD
ROAD A3095
Copperfield Av
Dovedale Cl
Hexham Cl
Way
Wasdale Cl
Magdalene Road
Merton Cl
Keble Wy
Yale Cl
Peterhouse Cl
Owlsmoor
Durham Rd
Rookwood Av
Oxford Rd
Trinity
Fakenham Wy
Keynsham Wy
Lewisham Wy
Acacia Av
Tottenham Wk
Union Cl
Church Road
Cambridge Rd
Owlsmoor Primary School
Nuffield Dr
Wdlnds Ct
Wadham
SANDHURST
Millins Cl
Avenue
Culver Rd
Road
Victoria Rd
Moor Cl
Birkbeck Pl
Balliol Way
Harvard Rd
Evesham Wk
Horsham Rd
Spring Woods
Ltl Moor
Compton Close
Apple Tree Wy
Oak
Yeovil Road
Surgery
PO
Girton Cl
Innes
Primrose Wy
Greenways
Broom Acres
Beech Ride
Robin Lane
Road
Abingdon Road
Cookham Cl
Faringdon Cl
Atrebatti Rd
May Cl
Owlsmoor
Whitmore Cl
Sandhurst School
Sandhurst Sports Centre
College Town
Sterling Gdns
Silver Hl
Hallmark Cl
Cannon Close
Orchard Ga
GU47
Pinehill Rl
Thibet Regents Pl
Farcrosse Cl
Hungerford Cl
Rother Cl
Isis Wy
Theal Cl
Wargrove Dr
Wantage Rd
Blackbird Cl
Blackcap Pl
College Town Inf & Jun Sch
Road
Hill
Range Vw
Brakes Rl
Wellington Rd
Evenlode Way
Severn Cl
St Marys Cl
Wellington Cl
Humber Wy
Crane Ct
Crake Pl
Avocet Crs
College Crs
The Close
Richmond Rd
Academy Pl
School
11
Albion Road
The Broadway
Gibbons Cl
Park Road
Brookside
Green La
Travis La
Wling Ter
Godfrey Cl
A3095
Premier Inn
Moray Av
Inverness Way
Kilmuir Cl
Cormorant Pl
Alxndr Cl
College Road
The Breech
Woodside
Hillside
Range Ride
A321
Surgery
YORKTOWN 30 ROAD
Sandhurst Sports Club
The Wellburn Cl
St John's Rd
Woodbine Close
Beaver Moss
Travis Lane
Florence Road
Branksome
Clarke Crs
Pine Cl
Road
Stubbs Folly
Devon Cl
Dalley Ct
Gower Pk
Davis Gdns
Westbourne Rd
Fairmead Cl
Egerton Road
Blackwater River
ogmore
Forbes Cha
Raeburn Way
Coxgreen
Burne-Jones Dr
Whistler Gv
Turner Pl
Yorktown Road
Munnings Dr
Cruikshank Lea
Fraser Md
Hogarth Cl
Landseer Cl
Fielding Rd
Egerton Rd
Oak Gv Crs
Birdwood Rd
Chapel Sq
White Road
Haig Rd
Governors Road
Lowry Cl
MARSHALL ROAD
Hearsey Gardens
Lyndhurst Av
Andover Dr
Christchurch Road
Rosemary Lane
Hearsey Gdns
Alton Ride
Burley Wy
Constable Wy
P
LC
Beaulieu Gdns
Christchurch Drive
Sandown
Binsted Dr
Fyfield Cl
20
Meadows (Superstores)
Laundry Lane
MARSHALL ROAD
Hicks La
Olde Farm Rd
Hartley Cl
Bramley La
Surgery
Foxley Cl
Rosemary Lane
Hamble Av
Cedar Av
Superstore
1 grid square represents 500 metres

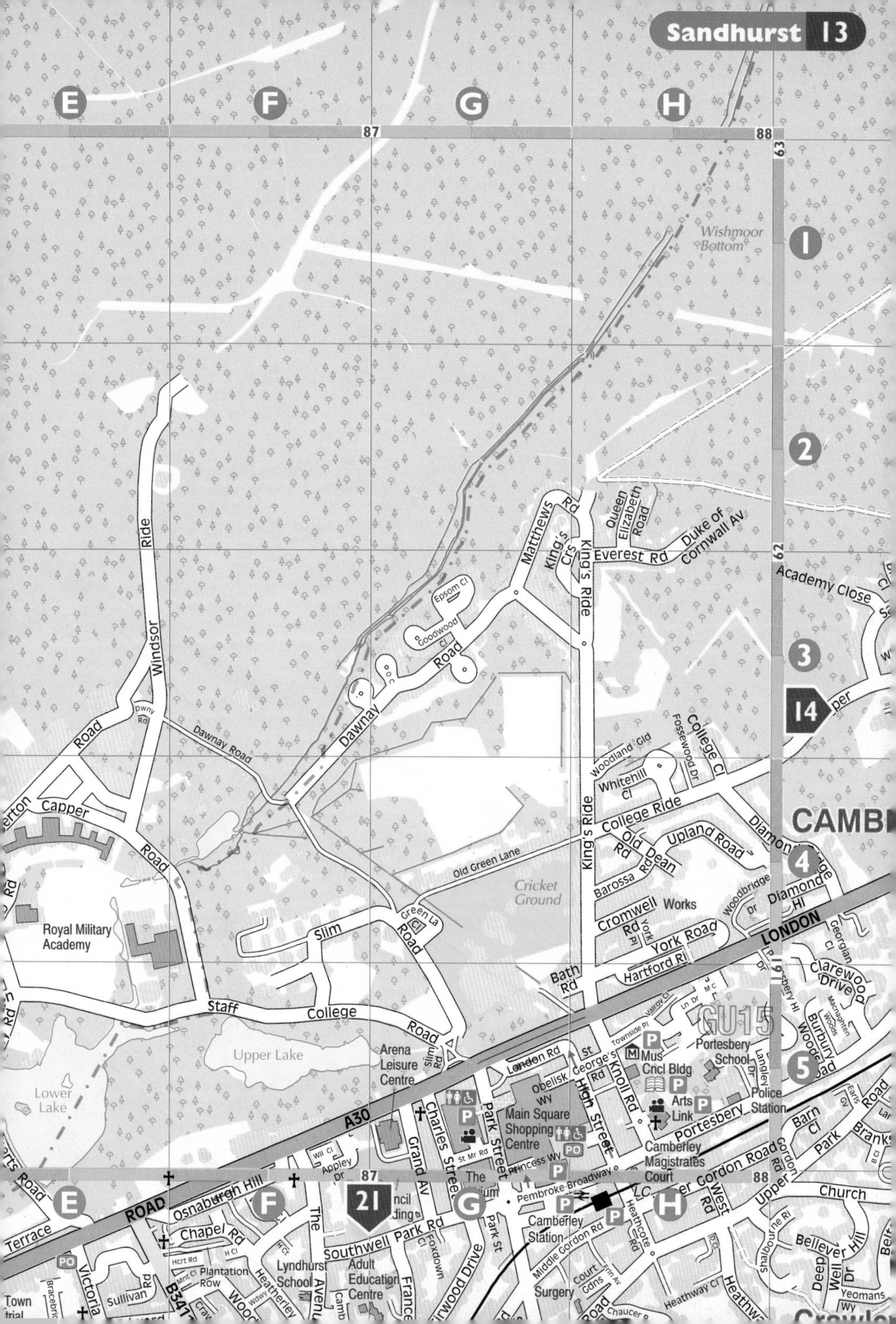

E
F
G
H
87
88
63
62
1
2
3
4
5
14
21
Wishmoor Bottom
Windsor Ride
Road
Dwny Rd
Dawnay Road
Capper Road
Royal Military Academy
Staff College Road
Upper Lake
Lower Lake
Dawnay Road
Epsom Cl
Goodwood Cl
Matthews Rd
King's Crs
King's Ride
Queen Elizabeth Road
Everest Rd
Duke of Cornwall Av
Academy Close
CAMB
Woodland Gld
Whitehill Cl
Fossewood Dr
College Cl
College Ride
Old Green Lane
Old Dean Rd
Upland Road
Diamond Ridge
Barossa Rd
Cricket Ground
Works
Cromwell Rd
York Pl
York Road
Woodbridge Dr
Diamond Hl
Hartford Ri
Bath Rd
Slim Road
Green La Cl
Slim Rd
Arena Leisure Centre
LONDON
A30
ROAD
A30
Georgian Cl
Clarewood Drive
Macnaghten Woods
Burbury Woods Road
Portesbery Hl
Valroy Cl
Ln Dr
M C
GU15
Townside Pl
London Rd
St George's Rd
Knoll Rd
Mus
Cncl Bldg
Arts Link
Portesbery School
Langley Dr
Police Station
Obelisk Wy
Main Square Shopping Centre
High Street
Park Street
Charles Street
Grand Av
St Mr Rd
Princess Wy
PO
Portesbery Rd
Camberley Magistrates Court
Upper Gordon Road
Gordon Rd
Barn Cl
Park Road
Branksome
Earls Gv
B Cl
Church
Wll Cl
Appley Dr
Osnaburgh Hill
Terrace Road
Chapel Rd
The Atrium
Pembroke Broadway
Camberley Station
LC
West Rd
Heathcote Rd
Middle Gordon Rd
Southwell Park Rd
The Avenue
Foxdown Cl
Park St
Hcrt Rd
H Cl
Mnt Cl
Plantation Row
Heatherley
Lyndhurst School
Adult Education Centre
Council Building
Surgery
Court Gdns
Frin Av
Heathway Cl
Heathway
Shalbourne Ri
Bellever Hill
Deep Well Dr
Yeomans Wy
Chaucer
Victoria
Sullivan Rd
Bracebridge
Town
B3411
Wdwy
Camb
France
Firwood Drive
PO

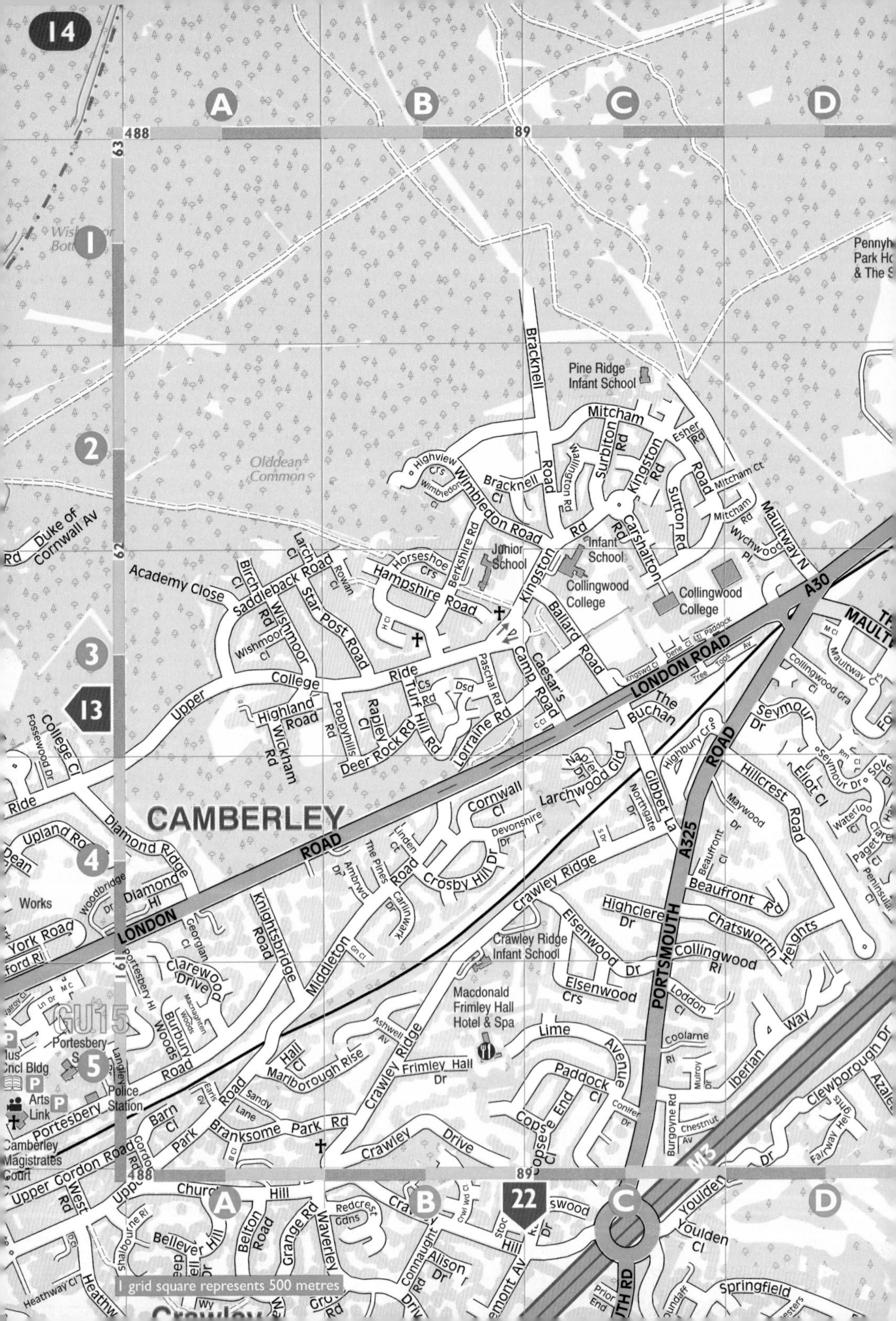
A
B
C
D
488
89
63
62
61
1
2
3
4
5
13
22
Wishmoor Bottom
Olddean Common
Pennyhill Park Hotel & The Spa
Bracknell Road
Pine Ridge Infant School
Mitcham Rd
Surbiton Rd
Kingston Rd
Esher Rd
Wallington Rd
Highview Crs
Wimbledon Cl
Wimbledon Road
Bracknell Cl
Sutton Rd
Carshalton Rd
Mitcham Ct
Maultway N
Wychwood Pl
Infant School
Junior School
Collingwood College
Duke of Cornwall Av
Academy Close
Larch Cl
Birch Cl
Saddleback Road
Rowan Cl
Horseshoe Crs
Berkshire Rd
Hampshire Road
Wishmoor Rd
Wishmoor Cl
Star Post Road
Ballard Road
Caesar's Camp Road
Kingston Rd
Upper College Ride
Highland Road
Wickham Rd
Poppyhills Rd
Rapley Cl
Deer Rock Rd
Turf Hill Rd
Paschal Rd
Lorraine Rd
London Road
A30
The Maultway
Tree Tops Av
The Buchan
Napier Dr
Larchwood Gld
Gibbet La
Northgate Dr
Highbury Crs
Collingwood Cl
Maultway Crs
Collingwood Gra
Seymour Dr
Hillcrest Road
Maywood Dr
Eliot Cl
Waterloo Cl
Paget Cl
Peninsular Cl
CAMBERLEY
College Cl
Fossewood Dr
Ride
Upland Road
Dean
Diamond Ridge
Diamond Hl
Woodbridge Dr
Works
York Road
Cornwall Cl
Devonshire Dr
Linden Ct
The Pines
Ambrwd Dr
Road
Crosby Hill Dr
Crawley Ridge
Carlinwalk Dr
Knightsbridge Road
Middleton Road
Georgian Cl
Portesbery Hl
Clarewood Drive
Burbury Woods
Woods Road
Macnaghten Woods
Crawley Ridge Infant School
Elsenwood Dr
Elsenwood Crs
Highclere Dr
Beaufront Cl
Beaufront Rd
Chatsworth Heights
Collingwood Ri
Loddon Cl
PORTSMOUTH ROAD
A325
GU15
Portesbery School
Langley
Mus
Cncl Bldg
Arts Link
Police Station
Camberley Magistrates Court
Portesbery Road
Macdonald Frimley Hall Hotel & Spa
Ashwell Av
Hall Cl
Marlborough Rise
Frimley Hall Dr
Lime Avenue
Coolarne Rl
Mulroy Dr
Iberian Way
Clewborough Dr
Azalea
Fairway Heights
Paddock Cl
Conifer Dr
Copse End
Copse Cl
Burgoyne Rd
Chestnut Av
M3
Barn Cl
Earls Gv
Sandy Lane
Park Road
Branksome Park Rd
Crawley Drive
Upper Gordon Road
Gordon Rd
West Rd
Church Hill
Belton Road
Grange Rd
Waverley
Redcrest Gdns
Connaught Rd
Alison Dr
Stoc Hill
Youlden Dr
Youlden Cl
Springfield
Shalbourne Rl
Bellever Hill
Heathway Cl
Heathw
Prior End
Crawley
1 grid square represents 500 metres

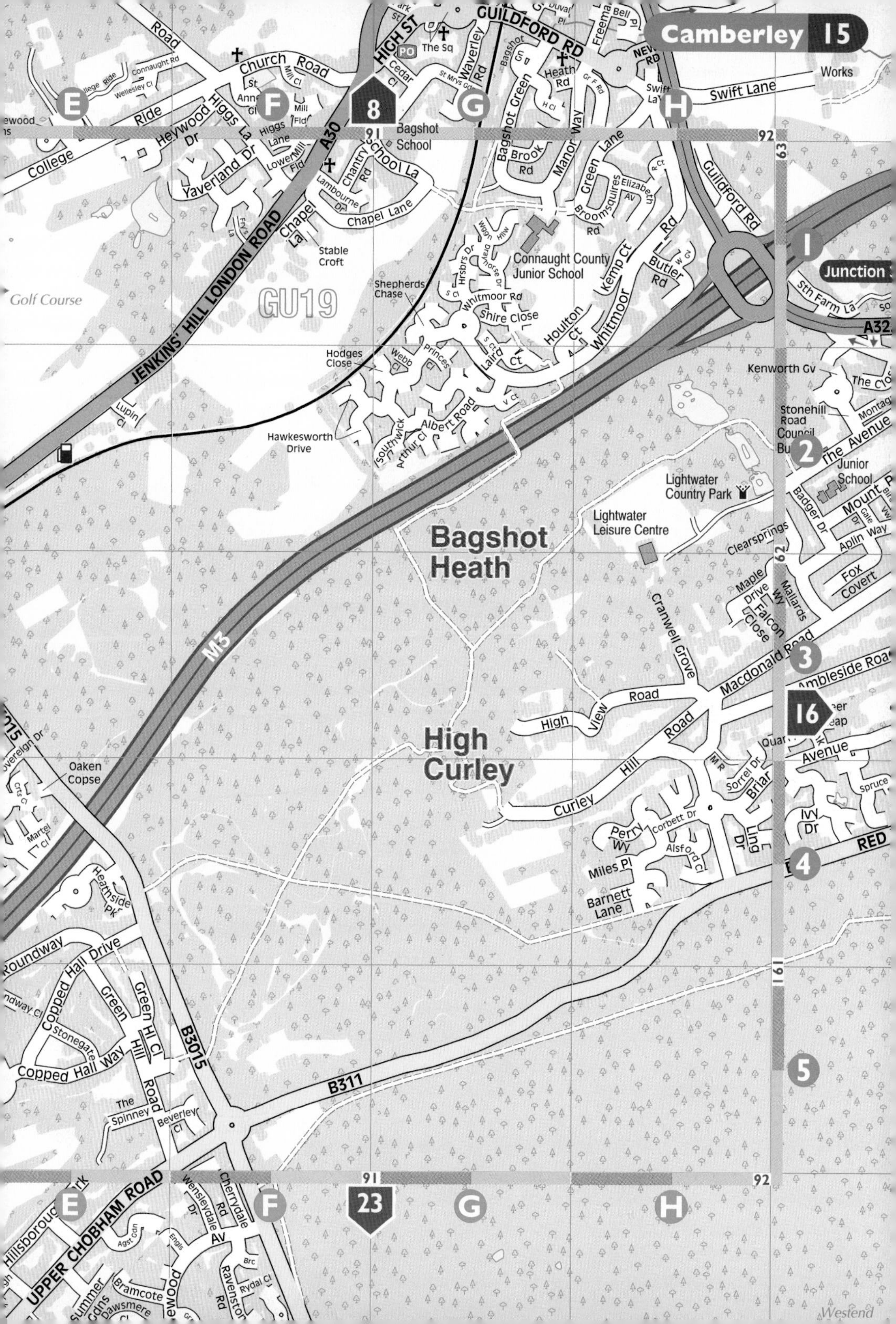
GUILDFORD RD
HIGH ST
The Sq
PO
Waverley Rd
Cedar
Church Road
Connaught Rd
Wellesley Cl
Heath Rd
Bell Pl
Swift Lane
Works
E
F
G
H
8
Bagshot School
School La
Chantry Rd
Lambourne Dr
Chapel Lane
Chapel La
Stable Croft
College Ride
Heywood Dr
Higgs La
Higgs Lane
Yaverland Dr
A30
JENKINS' HILL LONDON ROAD
Bagshot Green
Brook Rd
Manor Way
Green Lane
Broomsquires Rd
Elizabeth Av
Guildford Rd
Connaught County Junior School
Kemp Ct
Butler Rd
Whitmoor Rd
Shire Close
Houlton Ct
Whitmoor
Laird Ct
Princes
Webb Cl
Shepherds Chase
Hodges Close
Hawkesworth Drive
Albert Road
Southwick
Arthur Cl
Lupin Cl
Golf Course
GU19
Junction 3
Sth Farm La
A322
Kenworth Gv
The Close
Stonehill Road Council
The Avenue
Junior School
Lightwater Country Park
Lightwater Leisure Centre
Badger Dr
Mount Pl
Aplin Way
Fox Covert
Clearsprings
Maple Drive
Falcon Close
Mallards Wy
Macdonald Road
Ambleside Road
Cranwell Grove
Bagshot Heath
M3
High View Road
High Curley
Curley Hill Road
16
Avenue
Sorrel Dr
Briar
Spruce
Ivy Dr
Perry Wy
Corbett Dr
Alsford Cl
Ling Dr
Miles Pl
Barnett Lane
RED
Oaken Copse
Sovereign Dr
Martel Cl
Heathside Pk
Roundway
Copped Hall Drive
Green
Green Hl Cl
Hill Road
Stonegate
Copped Hall Way
B3015
The Spinney
Beverley Cl
B311
91
92
63
62
61
1
2
3
4
5
23
UPPER CHOBHAM ROAD
Hillsborough Pk
Wensleydale Dr
Cherrydale Rd
Av
Bramcote
Rydal Cl
Ravenstone Rd
Westend

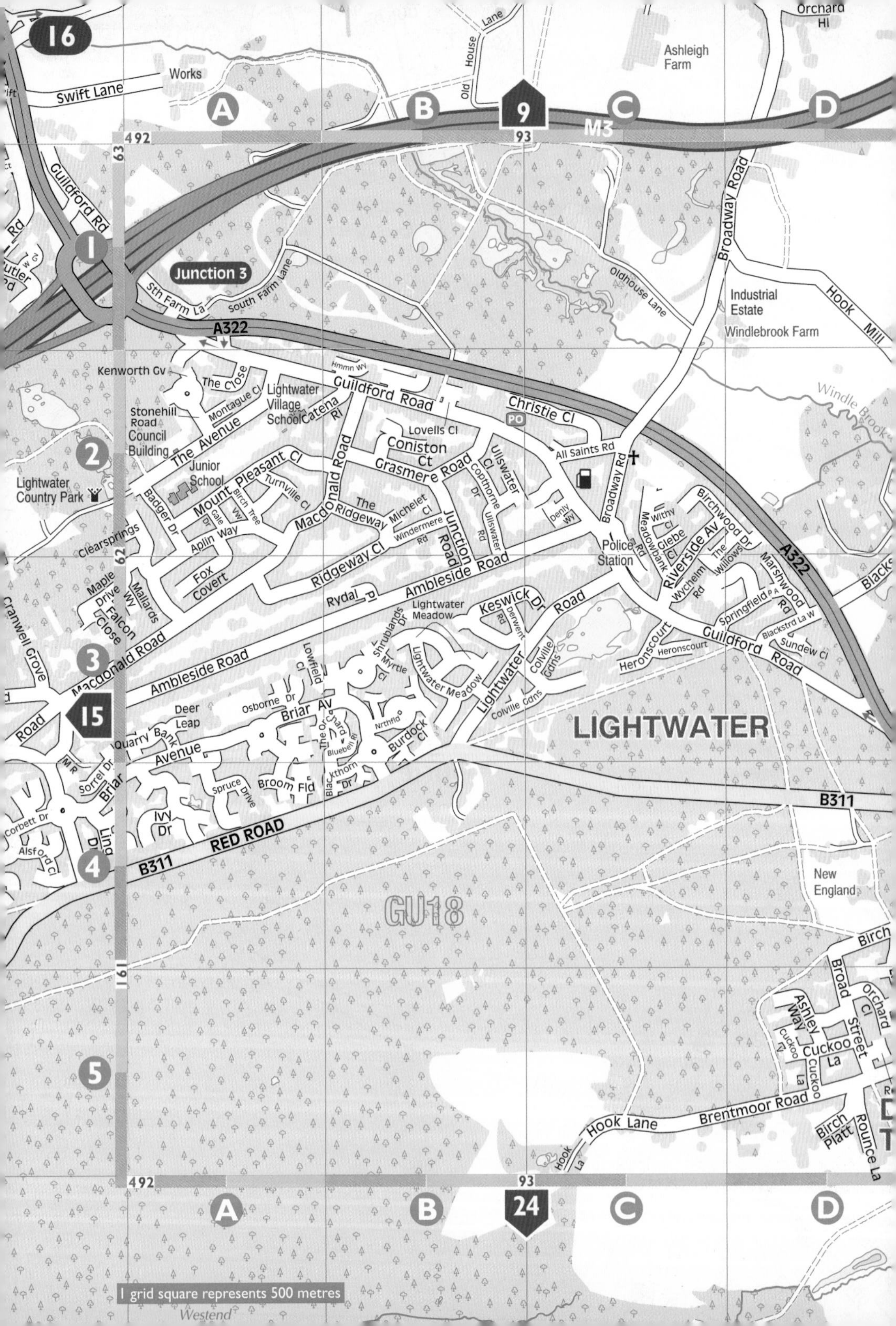

16
9
24
15
A
B
C
D
1
2
3
4
5
492
93
63
62
61
M3
A322
B311
Junction 3
LIGHTWATER
GU18
Swift Lane
Works
Old House Lane
Ashleigh Farm
Orchard Hl
Guildford Rd
Sth Farm La
South Farm Lane
Oldhouse Lane
Broadway Road
Industrial Estate
Windlebrook Farm
Hook Mill
Windle Brook
Kenworth Gv
The Close
Montague Cl
Lightwater Village School
Catena Ri
Guildford Road
Hmmn Wy
Christie Cl
PO
Stonehill Road Council Building
The Avenue
Junior School
Lightwater Country Park
Mount Pleasant Cl
Macdonald Road
Lovells Cl
Coniston Ct
Grasmere Road
Copthorne Dr
Ullswater Cl
All Saints Rd
Broadway Rd
Badger Dr
Gale Dr
Birch Tree Wy
Turnville Cl
The Ridgeway
Michelet Cl
Windermere Rd
Junction Road
Ullswater Rd
Denly Wy
Police Station
Meadowbank Rd
Withy Cl
Glebe Cl
Riverside Av
Birchwood Dr
The Willows
Marshwood Rd
Aplin Way
Clearsprings
Fox Covert
Ridgeway Cl
Ambleside Road
Maple Drive
Mallards Wy
Falcon Close
Rydal Pl
Lightwater Meadow
Keswick Dr
Derwent Rd
Road
Wychelm Rd
Springfield P A
Blackstrd La W
Sundew Cl
Heronscourt
Cranwell Grove
Macdonald Road
Ambleside Road
Lowfield Cl
Shrublands Dr
Myrtle Cl
Lightwater Meadow
Lightwater
Colville Gdns
Guildford Road
Blacks
Road
Deer Leap
Osborne Dr
Briar Av
The Orchard
Bluebell Ri
Nrthfld
Burdock Cl
Quarry Bank
Avenue
M R
Sorrel Dr
Briar
Spruce Drive
Broom Fld
Blackthorn Dr
Corbett Dr
Ivy Dr
Alsford Cl
Ling Dr
RED ROAD
New England
Birch
Broad Street
Orchard Cl
Ashley Way
Cuckoo Ly
Cuckoo La
Cuckoo La
Brentmoor Road
Hook Lane
Hook La
Birch Platt
Rounce La
1 grid square represents 500 metres
Westend

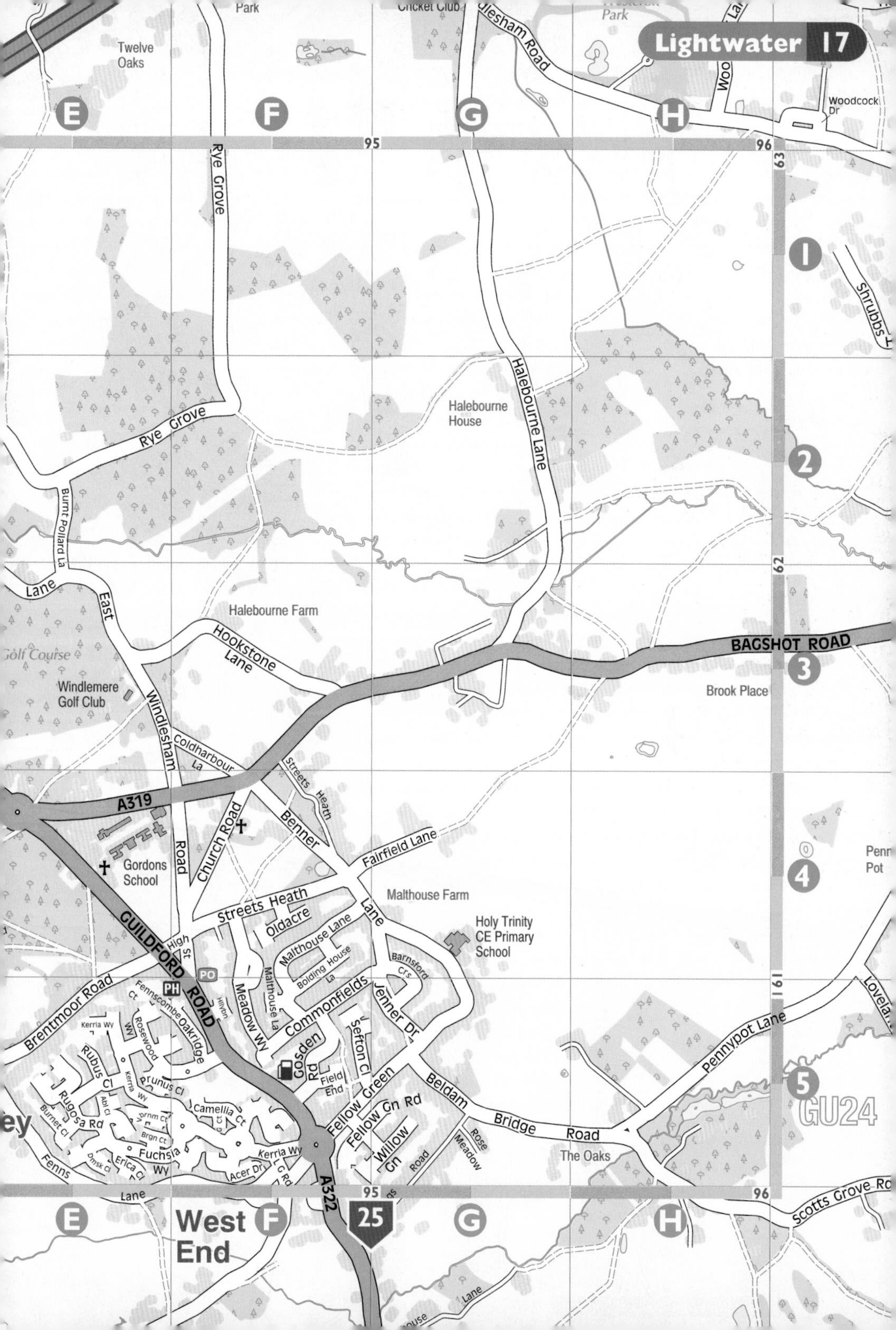
Twelve Oaks
Park
Cricket Club
Park
Windlesham Road
Woodcock Dr
E
F
G
H
I
95
96
63
62
61
Rye Grove
Shrubbs
Halebourne House
Halebourne Lane
Burnt Pollard La
Lane
East
Halebourne Farm
Hookstone Lane
BAGSHOT ROAD
Brook Place
Golf Course
Windlemere Golf Club
Windlesham Road
Coldharbour La
Streets Heath
A319
Church Road
Benner Lane
Fairfield Lane
Gordons School
Malthouse Farm
Holy Trinity CE Primary School
Streets Heath
Oldacre
Malthouse Lane
GUILDFORD ROAD
High St
PO
PH
Brentmoor Road
Fennscombe Ct
Oakridge
Kerria Wy
Rosewood
Meadow Wy
Malthouse La
Bolding House La
Barnsford Crs
Commonfields
Jenner Dr
Sefton Cl
Gosden Rd
Field End
Fellow Green
Fellow Gn Rd
Willow Gn
Road
Beldam Bridge Road
Rose Meadow
Pennypot Lane
Penny Pot
Loveland
Rubus Cl
Prunus Cl
Rugosa Rd
Camellia Ct
Burnet Cl
Fuchsia Wy
Erica Cl
Kerria Wy
Acer Dr
A322
The Oaks
GU24
Fenns Lane
West End
25
Scotts Grove Rd
Lane
1
2
3
4
5

Firgrove Road
Firgrove
Bramling Av
Aylesham
Partridge Av
Blakes Ride
Selwyn Dr
Colwyn Cl
Southwark Cl
Old School La
Macrae Rd
Lane
Health Centre
Lawford Crescent
Cranford
St Peter's Gdns
Yateley Infant S
GU46
Surgery
Lwr Canes
Monteagle La
Goldcrest Cl
Fieldfare Av
Swallow Way
Kingfisher Dr
Scott Pk
Hall
Home Park Rd
Parkfields
Drive
Tesimond Dr
T Crs
A
B
C
D
10
480
81
School
Yateley School
Westfields Infant School
Westfields Junior School
Holbeche Cl
Ryves Av
Tresham Crs
Morley Cl
Dunsmore Gdns
Oldcorne Hollow
Huddington Gld
Throgmorton Road
Garnet Fld
Catesby Gdns
Kits Croft
Monteagle Lane
Wistaria La
Minstead Dr
Farm View
Winton Crs
Drive
The Dell
Lymington Av
Byways
Hilltop Vw
Limecroft
Vigo La
Cullen Cl
Patten Av
Coppice Gdns
Hangerfield Cl
Hall Farm Crescent
Lucas Cl
Manor Park
Maple Gdns
Nutley Cl
Handford Lane
Greenhaven
Monteagle La
Shelley Wk
Dickens Wy
Newlands CP School
Dungells La
Newlands Cl
The Oaks
Mistletoe Rd
Wordsworth
The Sett
Cornfields
Gibbs Way
Keats Wy
Hardy
Avenue
Christie Walk
Mistletoe Cl
Stockbridge Way
Mlms Cl
Walnut Cl
Wordsworth Av
Herriot Court
Glwy Rd
Aragon Road
Wildwood Gdns
Freshwood Dr
Barton's Drive
Stookes Way
Harvest Close
Betjeman Walk
Blackbushe Business Park
Stoney Cl
Whitley Road
Drive
PO
Little Vigo
Saxony Wy
Dungells
Birchview Cl
Highwood Cl
Tuscany Way
Tudor
Woodlands
Vigo Lane
60
1
2
3
4
5
Works
Works
59
Blackbushe Airport
A30
Hartford Bridge Flats
B3013
West Minley Farm
158
13
28
Yateley Heath Wood
Minley Wood
1 grid square represents 500 metres

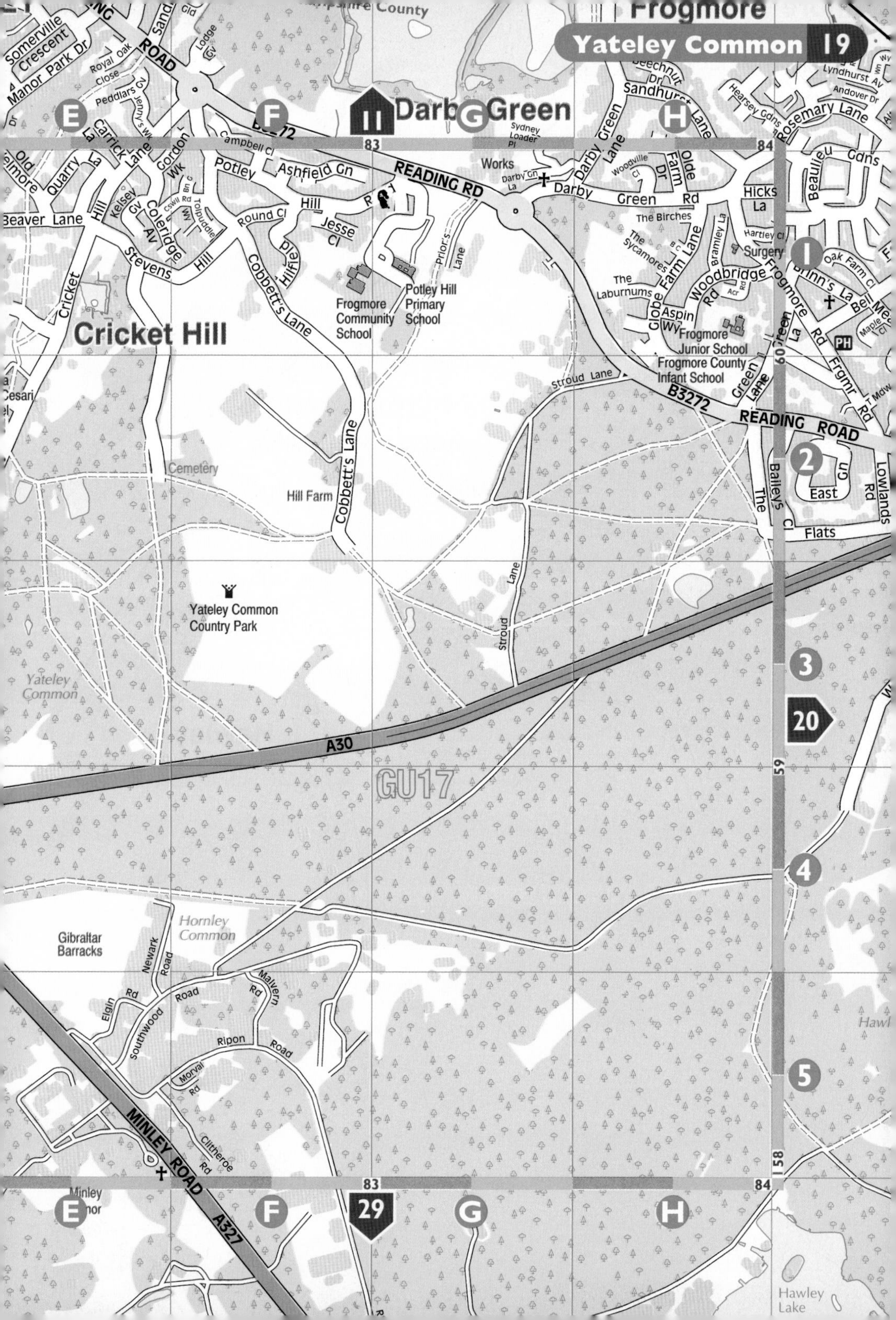
Frogmore
Darby Green
Cricket Hill
Yateley Common Country Park
Yateley Common
Hornley Common
Gibraltar Barracks
Hill Farm
Cemetery
Frogmore Community School
Potley Hill Primary School
Frogmore Junior School
Frogmore County Infant School
Works
Surgery
READING RD
READING ROAD
B3272
A30
A327
MINLEY ROAD
GU17
Cobbett's Lane
Stroud Lane
Prior's Lane
Potley Hill
Stevens Hill
Darby Green Rd
Darby Green Lane
Frogmore Rd
Globe Farm Lane
Woodbridge Rd
Green Lane
Flats
Lowlands Rd
East Gn
The Baileys Cl
Rosemary Lane
Sandhurst Lane
Olde Farm Dr
Hicks La
Beaulieu Gdns
Newark Road
Southwood Road
Ripon Road
Malvern Rd
Elgin Rd
Morval Rd
Clitheroe Rd
Hawley Lake
Minley Manor
E
F
G
H
83
84
2
3
4
5
58
59
60
20
29

Frogmore
20
Hearsey Gardens
Rosemary Lane
Christchurch Drive
Hicks La
Frogmore Junior School
Frogmore County Infant School
B3272
READING ROAD
Frogmore Rd
Green Lane
Meadow Wy
Foxley Cl
Rosemary Lane
Cedar Av
Kingsway
Parkhill Road
Martins Cl
Frogmore Park Drive
The Lake Side
Beech Dr
Lowlands Rd
East Gn
The Flats
Baileys Cl
A30
LONDON RD
Blackwater
London Rd
Blackwater Station
MARSHALL ROAD
A321
The Meadows (Superstores)
Superstore
Laundry Lane
White Hart Industrial Estate
Blackwater Industrial Estate
Tank Rd
Travelodge
Trafalgar Wy
Nelson Way
Stanhope Road
Lawrence Wy
Admiralty Way
Constable Wy
Egerton
White Road
Haig Rd
Meadow Cl
Waldorf Heights
Bloomsbury Wy
Savoy Gv
Birch Dr
Fir Drive
Cavendish Ct
Burlington Ct
Belgrave Court
Grosvenor Court
Queensbury Pl
Woodside
Willow La
Green La
Sheraton Close
New Rd
The Glebe
Vicarage Road
Oakfield Road
Pine Drive
Hawley CP School
Hawley Green
Blackwater & Hawley Leisure Centre
Hawley
Medlar Dr
Barberry Wy
HAWLEY ROAD
Hawley Park
Fernhill Road
Hawley Grove
Starve Acre
Hawley Common
Hawley Place School
Woodlands Wk
Woodlands Cl
Fernhill Lane
Fernhill Cl
Fernhill Primary School
Field Rd
All Saints Crs
Clayton Road
Rowans Close
Perring Avenue
Derry Rd
Chapel
Cold Harbour Lane
Ratcliffe
Linstead Road
The Findings
The Covert
North
1 grid square represents 500 metres
A
B
C
D
1
2
3
4
5
12
19
30
484
85
60
59
58

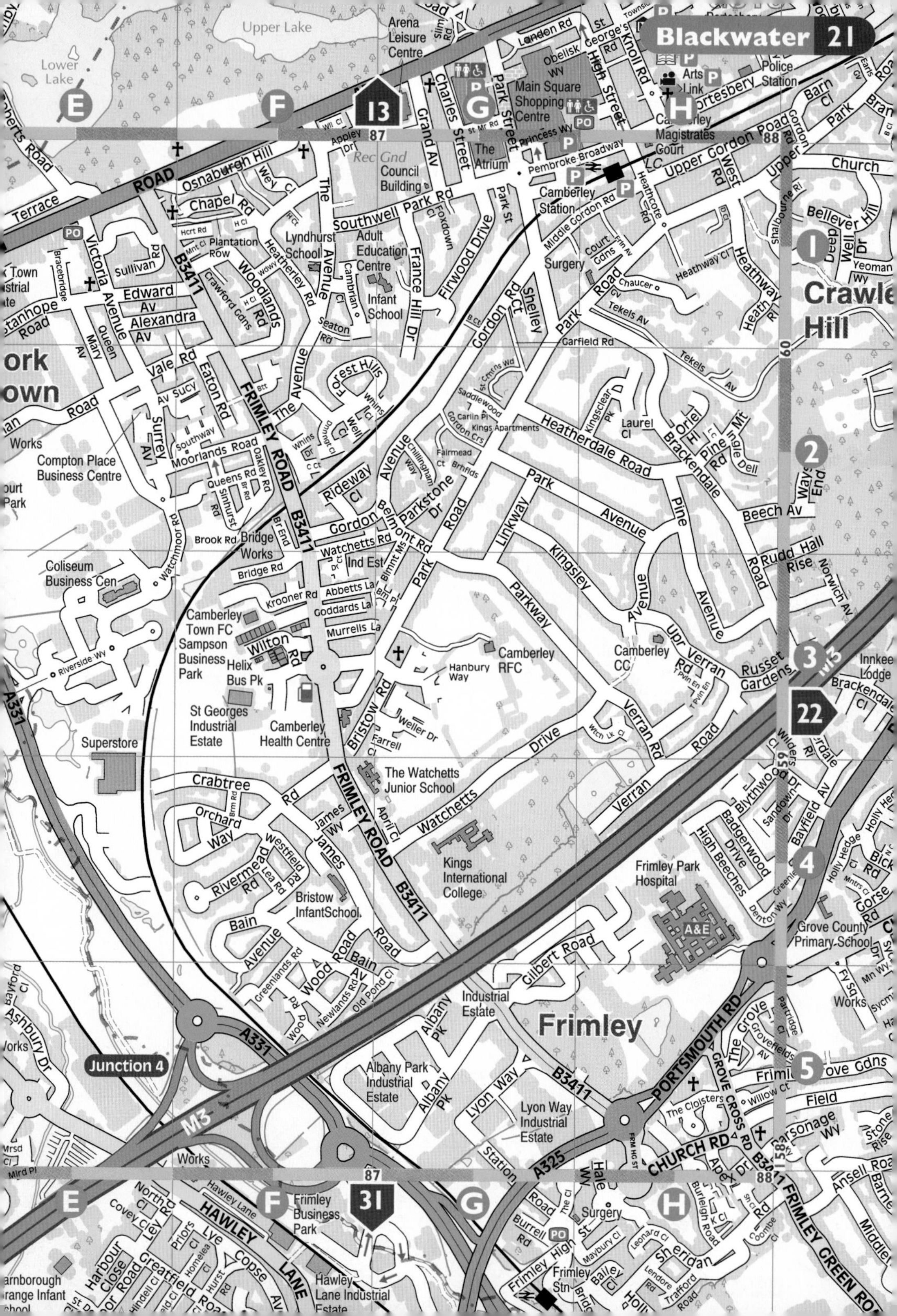

Blackwater 21
Upper Lake
Lower Lake
Arena Leisure Centre
13
Main Square Shopping Centre
High Street
Knoll Rd
London Rd
Obelisk Wy
Charles Street
Park Street
Grand Av
Princess Wy
The Atrium
Arts Link
Police Station
Portesbery Rd
Camberley Magistrates Court
Pembroke Broadway
Camberley Station
Upper Gordon Road
Gordon Rd
Barn Cl
Park
Church
Appley Dr
Rec Gnd
Council Building
Southwell Park Rd
Osnaburgh Hill
ROAD
Terrace
Chapel Rd
Wey Cl
The Avenue
Plantation Row
Lyndhurst School
Adult Education Centre
Infant School
Foxdown
France Hill Dr
Firwood Drive
Park St
Middle Gordon Rd
Heathcote Rd
West Rd
Shalbourne Ri
Bellever Hill
Deep Well Dr
Yeoman Wy
Crawley Hill
Heathway Cl
Heathway
Heath Ri
Surgery
Court Gdns
Chaucer Gv
Tekels Av
Garfield Rd
Victoria Avenue
Bracebridge
Sullivan Rd
Edward Av
Alexandra Av
Stanhope Road
Queen Mary Av
Crawford Gdns
Woodlands Rd
Heatherley Rd
Cambrian Cl
Seaton Rd
Shelley Ct
York Town
Industrial Estate
Vale Rd
Eaton Rd
Sucy Av
Surrey Av
Southway
Road
Works
Compton Place Business Centre
Moorlands Road
Oakley Rd
Queens Rd
Sinhurst Rd
FRIMLEY ROAD
B3411
Forest Hills
Whins Cl
Well Cl
Whins Dr
St Catherines Wd
Saddlewood
Carlin Pl
Kings Apartments
Gordon Crs
Heatherdale Road
Kingsclear Pk
Laurel Cl
Oriel Hl
Brackendale
Pine Rd
Mt Ingle Dell
2
Ways End
Beech Av
Chillingham Way
Fairmead Ct
Rideway Cl
Avenue
Parkstone Dr
Belmont Rd
Gordon
Park Avenue
Linkway
Kingsley Avenue
Pine Avenue
Road
Rudd Hall Rise
Norwich Av
Court Park
Watchmoor Rd
Brook Rd
Bridge Works
Watchetts Rd
Ind Est
Bridge Rd
Coliseum Business Cen
Krooner Rd
Abbetts La
Goddards La
Murrells La
Park Rd
Parkway
Upr Verran Rd
Camberley CC
Camberley Town FC
Sampson Business Park
Helix Bus Pk
Wilton Rd
Riverside Wy
Hanbury Way
Camberley RFC
Russet Gardens
3
M3
Innkeeper Lodge
Brackendale Cl
22
Bristow Rd
Weller Dr
Farrell Cl
St Georges Industrial Estate
Camberley Health Centre
Superstore
A331
Verran Rd
Watchetts Drive
Verran Road
Wilders Cl
Blythwood Dr
Sandown Dr
Bayfield Av
Crabtree Rd
Orchard Way
The Watchetts Junior School
James Wy
April Cl
Watchetts
Badgerwood Drive
High Beeches
Holly Hedge
Gorse Rd
Westfield Rd
Rivermead Rd
Lea Rd
James Rd
Kings International College
Frimley Park Hospital
A&E
4
Denton Wy
Grove County Primary School
Bristow Infant School
Bain Avenue
Bain Av
Greenlands Rd
Wood Road
Old Pond Cl
Newlands Rd
Gilbert Road
Industrial Estate
Albany Pk
Frimley
PORTSMOUTH RD
The Grove
Grovefields Av
Partridge Cl
Works
Bayford Cl
Ashbury Dr
Junction 4
A331
Albany Park Industrial Estate
Lyon Way
Lyon Way Industrial Estate
B3411
5
Frimley Grove Gdns
Field
Willow Ct
The Cloisters
GROVE CROSS RD
Parsonage Wy
Stone Rise
Station
A325
CHURCH RD
Works
Mird Pl
87
88
E
F
G
H
I
31
Frimley Business Park
Hale Wy
Surgery
Apex Dr
Burleigh Road
Ansell Road
FRIMLEY GREEN ROAD
North Cl
Ley Rd
Covey Cl
HAWLEY LANE
Hawley Lane
Priors Cl
Lye Copse Av
Homelea Cl
Hurst Rd
Harbour Close
Greatfield Road
Farnborough Grange Infant School
Hawley Lane Industrial Estate
Burrell Rd
PO
Frimley High St
Maybury Cl
Leonard Cl
Sheridan Rd
Bailey Cl
Frimley Stn
Lendore Rd
Trafford Rd

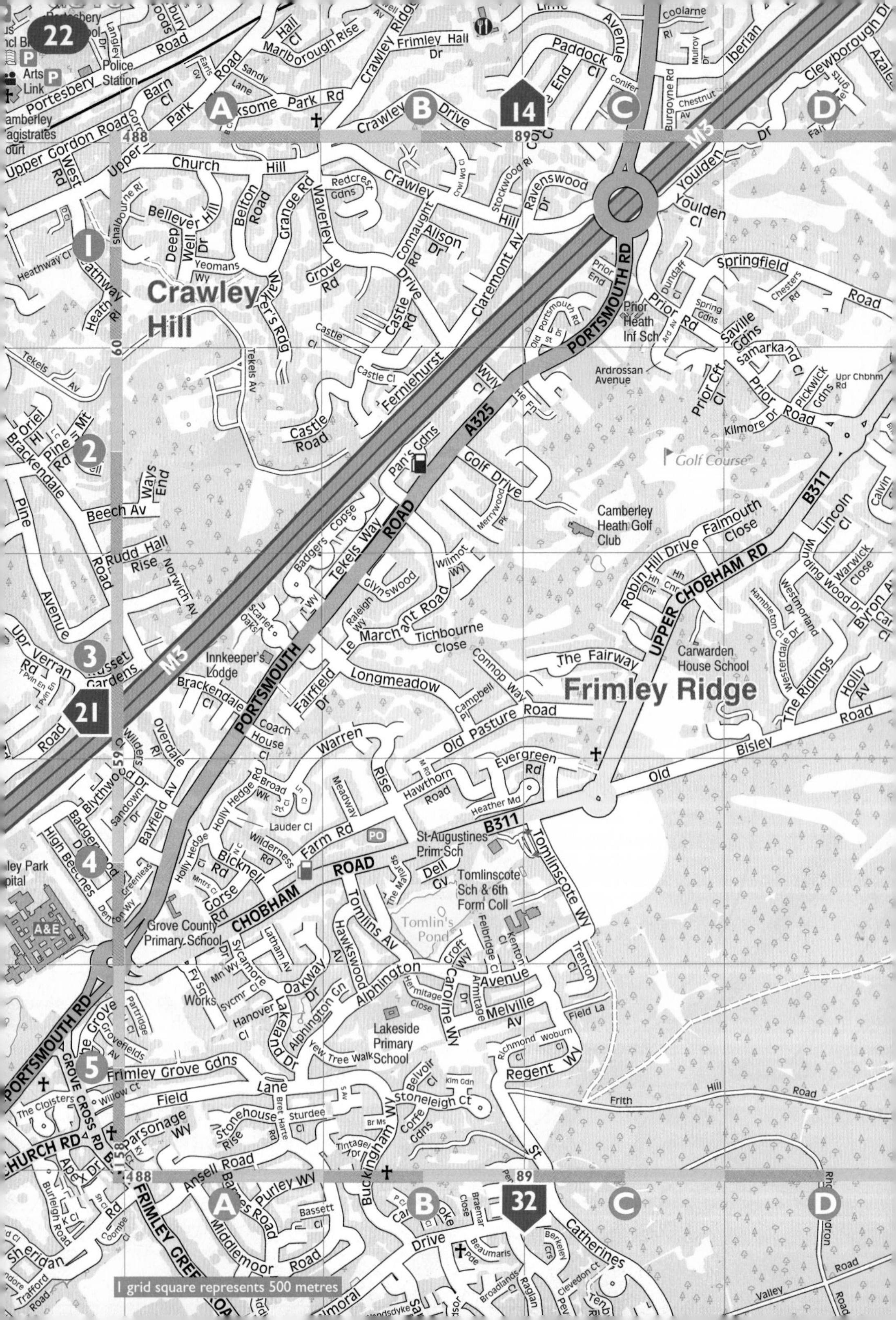
22
14
21
32
A
B
C
D
1
2
3
4
5
488
89
60
59
58
Crawley Hill
Frimley Ridge
M3
A325
B311
PORTSMOUTH RD
PORTSMOUTH ROAD
UPPER CHOBHAM RD
CHOBHAM ROAD
CHURCH RD
GROVE CROSS RD
FRIMLEY GREEN ROAD
Portesbery Road
Police Station
Arts Link
Camberley Magistrates Court
Upper Gordon Road
Upper Church Hill
West Rd
Park Road
Branksome Park Rd
Marlborough Rise
Frimley Hall Dr
Crawley Ridge
Crawley Drive
Crawley Hill
Paddock Cl
Avenue
Coolarne Ri
Iberian
Burgoyne Rd
Chestnut Av
Clewborough Dr
Youlden Dr
Youlden Cl
Ravenswood Dr
Stockwood Ri
Claremont Av
Connaught Rd
Alison Dr
Waverley
Grove Rd
Redcrest Gdns
Grange Rd
Belton Road
Bellever Hill
Deep Well Dr
Yeomans Wy
Walker's Rdg
Shalbourne Ri
Heathway Cl
Heathway
Heath Ri
Castle Cl
Castle Rd
Castle Road
Drive
Ferniehurst
Tekels Av
Prior End
Old Portsmouth Rd
Springfield Road
Dundaff Cl
Prior Rd
Spring Gdns
Chesters Rd
Prior Heath Inf Sch
Saville Gdns
Samarkand Cl
Ardrossan Avenue
Prior Cft Cl
Pickwick Gdns
Upr Chbhm Rd
Prior Road
Kilmore Dr
Golf Course
Golf Drive
Merrywood Pk
Pan's Gdns
Camberley Heath Golf Club
Falmouth Close
Robin Hill Drive
Lincoln Cl
Calvin
Winding Wood Dr
Warwick Close
Westmorland Dr
Hambleton Cl
Westerdale Dr
Byron Av
Carwarden House School
The Ridings
Holly Av
Road
The Fairway
Old Bisley Road
Oriel Hl
Pine Mt
Brackendale
Pine Avenue
Ways End
Beech Av
Rudd Hall Rise
Road
Norwich Av
Badgers Copse
Tekels Way
Glynswood
Wilmot Wy
Le Marchant Road
Tichbourne Close
Scarlet Oaks
Upr Verran Rd
Russet Gardens
Innkeeper's Lodge
Brackendale Cl
Fairfield Dr
Longmeadow
Connop Way
Campbell Pl
Old Pasture Road
Coach House Cl
Warren Rise
Evergreen Rd
Wilders Cl
Overdale Ri
Blythwood Dr
Sandown Dr
Bayfield Av
Holly Hedge Rd
Broad Wk
Meadway
Hawthorn Road
Heather Md
Badgers Dr
High Beeches
Lauder Cl
Farm Rd
PO
St Augustines Prim Sch
Tomlinscote Wy
Wilderness Rd
Bicknell Rd
Gorse Rd
The Marshes
Dell Cv
Tomlinscote Sch & 6th Form Coll
Frimley Park Hospital
A&E
Grove County Primary School
Tomlins Av
Tomlin's Pond
Latham Av
Sycamore
Hawkswood Av
Oakway Dr
Alphington Avenue
Croft Wy
Felbridge Cl
Kenton Cl
Trenton Cl
Armitage Dr
Caroline Wy
Melville Av
Field La
Hermitage Close
Alphington Gn
Lakeland Dr
Hanover Cl
Works
Partridge Cl
Grovefields Av
Lakeside Primary School
Yew Tree Walk
Richmond Cl
Woburn Cl
Regent Wy
Frimley Grove Gdns
Field Lane
Willow Ct
The Cloisters
Stonehouse Rise
Sturdee Cl
Bret Harte Rd
Belvoir Cl
Stoneleigh Ct
Corfe Gdns
Frith Hill Road
Parsonage Wy
Tintagel Dr
Buckingham Wy
St
Ansell Road
Barnes Road
Purley Wy
Middlemoor Road
Bassett Cl
Braemar Close
Drive
Beaumaris Pde
Broadlands
Raglan
Berkeley Crs
Clevedon Ct
Catherines
Burleigh Road
Sheridan Rd
Trafford Road
Valley Road
Road
1 grid square represents 500 metres

Copped Hall Way
The Spinney
Beverley Cl
B3015
B311
E
F
15
G
H
91
92
UPPER CHOBHAM ROAD
Hillsborough Park
Wensleydale Dr
Cherrydale Rd
Av
Ravenstone Rd
Rydal Cl
Buttermere Dr
Summer Gdns
Bramcote
Dawsmere Cl
Inglewood
Westend Common
Langdon Close
Norton Road
Tremayne Walk
Mardale
Inglewood Av
Eskdale Way
Keswick Cl
Copelands Close
Drive
Kendal Gv
Surgery
Cumberland Road
Arundel Road
PO
Heather Ridge County Infant School
Roxburgh Close
Bellingham Cl
Cheviot Close
Martindale Avenue
Brandon Cl
Pendragon Way
Kirkstone Close
Redwood Drive
THE MAULTWAY
Strawberry Bottom
eatherside
Coniston Close
Shildon Cl
Yockley Close
Herrick Cl
Silver Drive
Drive
Edgemoor Rd
Barbon Close
Ripon Close
Theobalds Way
Dalston Close
Mgr Dr
Maguire Dr
Ridgewood Dr
Cheylesmore Drive
Wingfield Gdns
Old Bisley Road
B3015
Habershon Dr
Pine Ridge Golf Club
Colony Gate
Golf Course
DEEPCUT BRIDGE ROAD
Minorca Av
Minorca Road
Aisne Road
I
2
3
24
4
5
60
59
58
Frith Hill Road
Valley Road
Drifters Dr
Durham Dr
Crofters Cl
B3015
33
Swrdsmn's Road
Earl
Chester Dr
Brock Cl
Suffolk Ct
Straw Ct
Cyprus Rd
Alma Gardens
Malta Road
Canada Rd
Dettingen Road
Newfound
BR RD

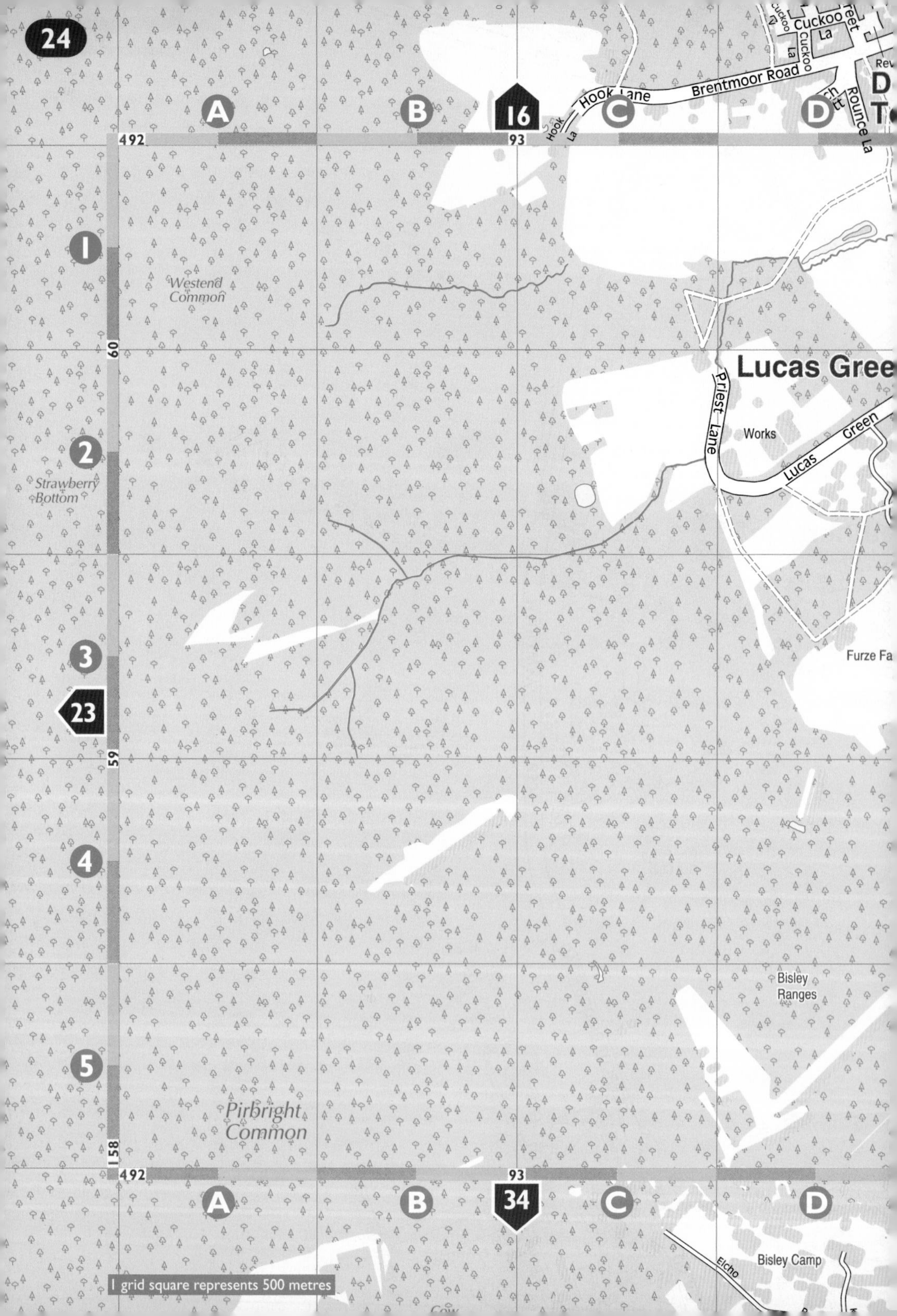
16
Cuckoo
Cuckoo La
La
Street
Brentmoor Road
Hook Lane
Hook La
Rounce La
A
B
C
D
492
93
1
Westend Common
60
Lucas Green
Priest Lane
Works
Lucas Green
2
Strawberry Bottom
3
23
Furze Fa
59
4
Bisley Ranges
5
Pirbright Common
158
34
Elcho
Bisley Camp
1 grid square represents 500 metres

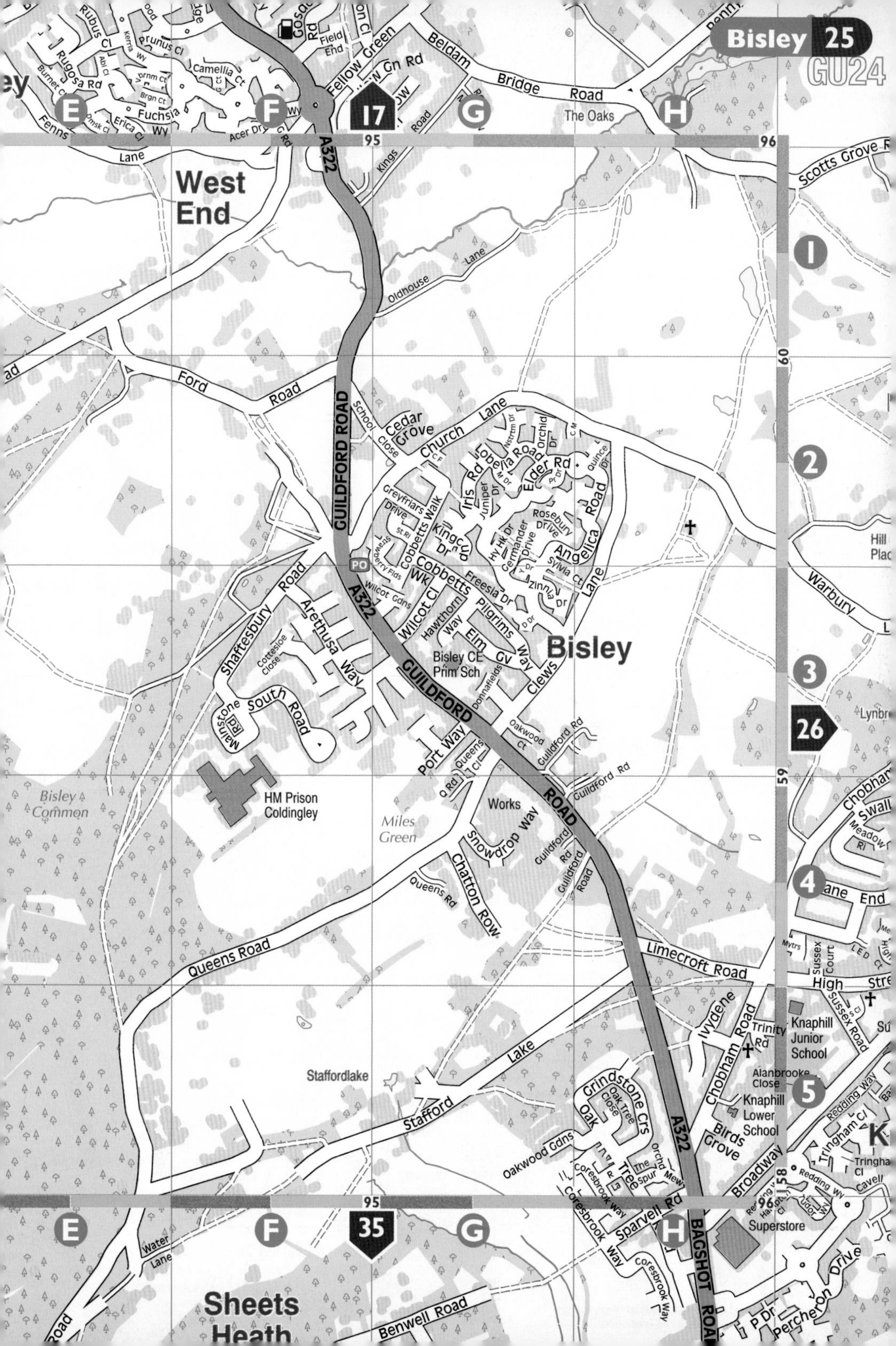
West End
Bisley
Sheets Heath
Bisley Common
Miles Green
Staffordlake
The Oaks
HM Prison Coldingley
Bisley CE Prim Sch
Works
Knaphill Junior School
Knaphill Lower School
Superstore
GUILDFORD ROAD
A322
BAGSHOT ROAD
Ford Road
Oldhouse Lane
Church Lane
Queens Road
Stafford Lake
Limecroft Road
Beldam Bridge Road
Shaftesbury Road
South Road
Arethusa Way
Cobbetts Walk
Pilgrims Way
Clews Lane
Angelica Road
Elder Rd
Lobelia Road
Iris Rd
Kingcup Dr
Rosebury Drive
Germander Drive
Sylvia Ct
Zinnia Dr
Freesia Dr
Wilcot Cl
Hawthorn Way
Elm Gv
Donnafields
Port Way
Queens Cl
Oakwood Ct
Snowdrop Way
Chatton Row
Queens Rd
Greyfriars Drive
Cedar Grove
School Close
Cottesloe Close
Mainstone Rd
Grindstone Crs
Oak Tree Close
Oakwood Gdns
Coresbrook Way
Sparvell Rd
Orchd Mews
The Spur
Ivydene
Chobham Road
Trinity Rd
Alanbrooke Close
Birds Grove
Broadway
Percheron Drive
Redding Way
Tringham Cl
Benwell Road
Water Lane
Warbury Lane
Scotts Grove Rd
Sussex Road
Sussex Court
High Street
Lane End
Meadow Ri
Fellow Green
Kings Road
Fenns Lane
Acer Dr
Fuchsia Wy
Erica Cl
Rugosa Rd
Camellia Ct
Prunus Cl
Rubus Cl
Field End
95
96
60
59
58
17
26
35

26
GU24
Castle Green
Millbrook
Scotts Grove Rd
Carthouse Lane
Knaphill Manor
Chobham Road
Chobham Golf Club
Golf Course
Garden Cent
Hill Place
Warbury Lane
Barr's Lane
Littlewick Road
Lynbrook
25
Knaphill
High Street
Knaphill Junior School
Knaphill Lower School
Alanbrooke Close
Oak Tree Clinic
Beaufort Primary School
St Johns CP School
The Winston Churchill School
The Lansbury Estate
Superstore
Woking St John's Crematorium
St Hugh of Lincoln RCP School
AMSTEL WAY
BAGSHOT ROAD
A322
36
1 grid square represents 500 metres

Heather Farm
Cox Hill
Coxhill Green
Deep Pool
E
F
G
H
I
99
500
CHOBHAM ROAD
A3046
Horsell Common Road
Littlewick Road
South Road
Common Cl
Cheapside
Carthouse Lane
Viggory Lane
Heather Cl
Russell Close
Russell Road
Horsell Birch
Bedford Close
Thornash Close
Thornash Road
Thornash Way
Grobars Av
Morton Road
Morton Close
Woking High School
Horsell Rise
Horsell Rise Close
Fairlawn Pk
Kettlewell Cl
Lindvale
The Limes
Ridgeway Gdns
Ridgeway Cl
Hammond Road
Hammond Close
Meadway Drive
Elm Close
Hill Cl
Horsell CE Junior School
Horsell
Southcote
Beech Gardens
Church Rd
Horsell Vale
Watts Lea
Darvel Cl
Claydon Road
Tresta Walk
Kestrel Way
GU21
The Orchard
Bullbeggars Lane
Nursery Close
Horsell Way
Whopshott Avenue
Whopshott Close
Rosehill Avenue
Ormonde Road
High Street
South Close
PO
Manor Road
Midsummer Wk
Pares Cl
Wilson Way
St Andrew's School
Church Cl
Horsell Pk
Graylands
Graylands Close
Woodstock Close
Horsell Moor
Horsell Park Close
Horsell Pk
Cem
Goldsworth Park Trading Estate
Cygnet Cl
Goldsworth Park
Willowmead Close
Sythwood
Brookfield
Primary School
Bury Lane
Bury Close
Langdale Cl
Infant Sch
Church Hill
Lych Way
Old Malt Way
Waldens Park Road
Pine Close
Tower Cl
Achilles Place
Well Close
Well Lane
Kirby Road
Waldens Road
K Rd
Holyoake Avenue
Holyoake Cr's
St Mary's Rd
Thomas Cl
Brewery Road
Surgery
Abbey Road
Woking & Horsell CC
Arthur's Br Road
Horsell Moor
Rhoda Theatre
New Victoria Theatre
Peacock Cinema
The Peacock Shop Cen
Brewery
Tresillian Wy
Veryan
Cardingham
Upton
Watercress Way
Quintrell Cl
French's Wells
Cobbetts Close
Colliers Close
Colliers Cl
Merrivale Gdns
Marston Road
Hallington Cl
Rofford
Ridsdale Road
Eastmead
Venton Cl
Torridon Cl
Trenance
Baintion Mead
Armadale
Perleybrooke La
Goldsworth Park Health Centre
Way
Hamble Cl
Ainsdale Way
Bampton
Halley's Ap
Alterton Cl
Fairbourne Cl
Fenwick Close
Westmead
Hedgerley Ct
Harelands Close
WellPath
Bridge Cl
Bridge Court
Goldsworth Rd Industrial Est
A324
LOCKFIELD DRIVE
Premier Inn
Bridge Ms
Mabel Street
Goldsworth Road
Works
Farm Rd
Oak's Rd
Hogan Bus Cen
Goldsworth Rd
Poole Rd
Butts Rd
Caradon Cl
Dene Place
Foxhills
Parley Drive
Goldsworth CP Sch
Avonmead
Bridge Barn Lane
Brambledene Cl
Surrey History Centre
Kingsway
Kingsway Av
Rosewarne Close
Denvale Wk
Thursby Rd
Elsdon Rd
Abercorn Way
Muirfield Rd
Greythorne Road
Shilburn Way
Chirton Wk
DRIVE
Wyndham Rd
Bankside
Waterside Way
Leafield
Helmsdale
Winnington Way
Glendale Cl
Abingdon Cl
Fairmead
Silversmiths Wy
De Lara Way
Elm Rd
Royal Oak Rd
York Road
LOCKFIELD
St James Cl
Cedar Gdns
Falstone
Inglewood
Colyton Cl
Wilders Cl
Badgers Cl
Greenham Wk
The Triangle
Triggs
Erica Ct
Dianthus Ct
Clover Ct
Pk
Pantiles Cl
St John's Rd
St John's Road
Martin Way
Dale Vw
Priors Ct
Woodend Close
Firgrove Hill
Barricane
St John's Rise
37
Janoway Hill La
The Dell
Birch Cl
Trigg's Cl
Trigg's Lane
Cavendish Road
Hill
Azalea
Mount Hermon Road
West Hill
Midhope Rd
Brooklyn Road
Tamerton Sq
Everlands Close
Lampeter
Belgrave Mnr
Greenfield Sch
A320
St Johns
St John's Hill
Church Rd
Jackman's Lane
Jackman's La
Holly Close
Firbank Drive
Firbank Lane
St Catherines
College Lane
Cinder Path
Glenlee
Alice Ruston Place
Wych Hill
York Road
Works
158
159
160
1
2
3
4
5

West Minley Farm
18
A
B
C
D
480
81
B3013
Blackbushe Farm
Blackbushes Road
Lichett Plain
Rotten Green Road
Turner's Green Lane
Pale Lane
Brook House
Broomhurst Farm
M3
Elvetham Heath Way
Ancells Rd
Barley Wy
Whitewater Rd
Winta Drive
Waleron Road
Elvetham Heath Local Nature Reserve
Fleet Service Area
Elvetham Heath
North Hants Golf Club
MINLEY RD
Tamworth Drive
Guernsey Dr
Golf Course
COVE RD
A3013 MINLEY ROAD
Old Cove Rd
Waterside Court
Fleet Station
Days Inn Hotel
Turgis Road
Marrow Mead
Elvetham Heath Wy
Turners Way
Wintney St
The Key
1 grid square represents 500 metres
39

MINLEY ROAD
A327
Minley Manor
Morval Rd
Clitheroe Rd
Ripon Road
Home Farm
MINLEY RD
Hawley Lake
Minley Rd
Junction 4a
30
19
40
M3
Bramshot Lane
Great Bramshott Farm
Innkeeper's Lodge
Ancells Road
Oasthouse Dr
Drovers End
Falkners Cl
Comm Cen
Hanover Dr
Forest Dean
Shire Av
Fernhill Tutors
Sankey La
FLEET ROAD
B3014
FLEET
Southwood Lane
A3013
Howard Dr
Lyndsey Cl
Fennel Cl
Tarragon Cl
Sorrel Cl
Broadhurst
Trunk Road
Burge Cl
Whetstone Rd
Brownsover
Rindle Cl
Pystck Crs
Columbus Drive
Old Wood Chase
Larch Way
Summit Av
Chamomile Gdns
Thyme Ct
Southwood

1 grid square represents 500 metres

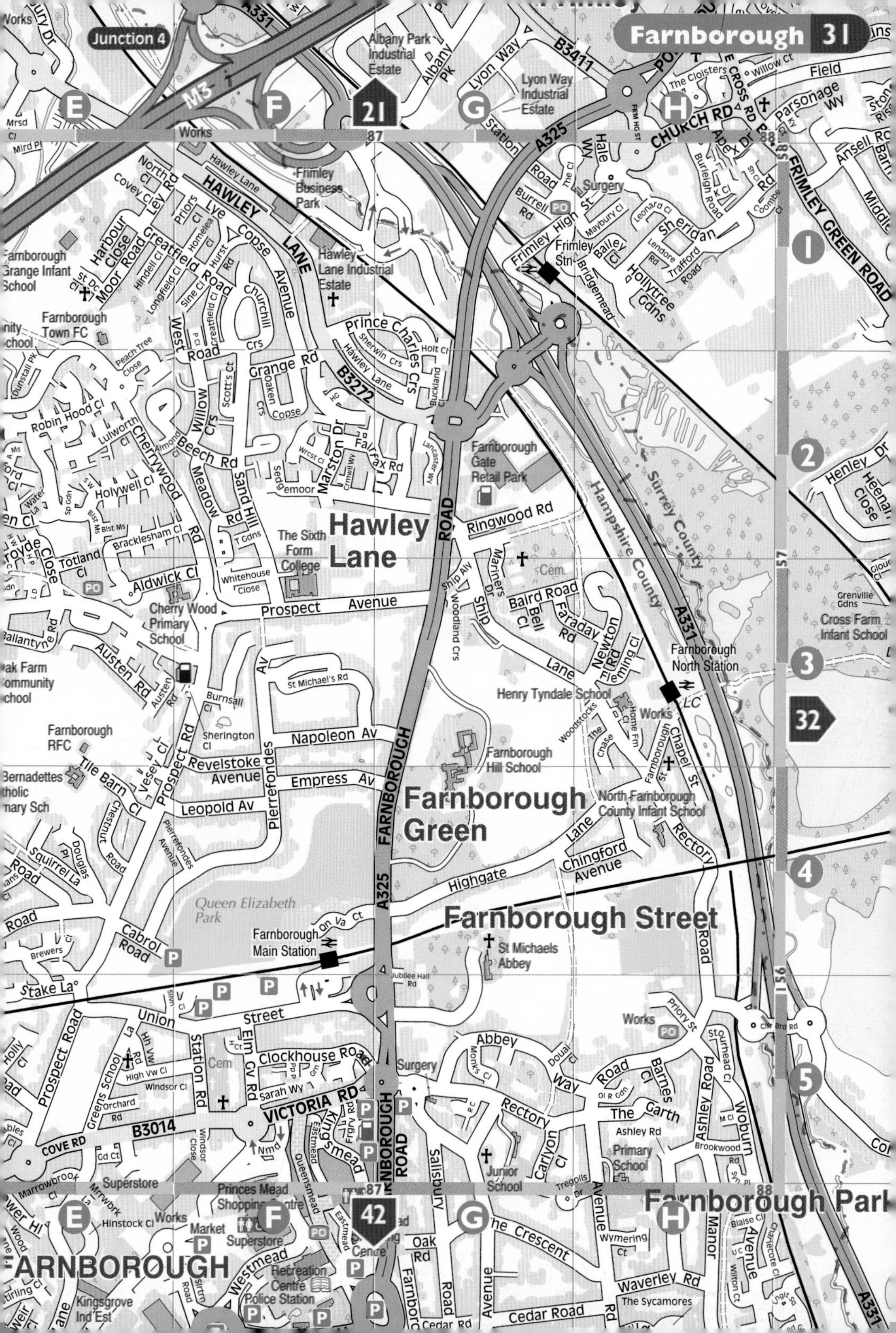

Junction 4
M3
A331
Albany Park Industrial Estate
21
Lyon Way
Lyon Way Industrial Estate
B3411
The Cloisters
Willow Ct
Field
CHURCH RD
Parsonage Wy
Works
87
88
Hawley Lane
HAWLEY LANE
Frimley Business Park
Hawley Lane Industrial Estate
Station Road
A325
Burrell Rd
Frimley High St
Surgery
Maybury Cl
Sheridan Rd
Burleigh Road
Frimley Stn
Bridgemead
Hollytree Gdns
Trafford Road
FRIMLEY GREEN ROAD
North Cl
Ley Rd
Covey Cl
Priors
Lye Copse Avenue
Homelea Cl
Harbour Close
Moor Road
Greatfield Road
Hurst Rd
Farnborough Grange Infant School
Longfield Cl
Churchill Crs
Farnborough Town FC
West Road
Prince Charles Crs
Sherwin Crs
Holt Cl
Peach Tree Close
Grange Rd
B3272
Buckland Cl
Oaken Copse Crs
Scott's Ct
Willow Crs
Robin Hood Cl
Lulworth
Cherrywood Rd
Beech Rd
Marston Dr
Fairfax Rd
Farnborough Gate Retail Park
Holywell Cl
Meadow Rd
Sand Hill
Sedgemoor
Ringwood Rd
Henley Dr
Heenan Close
Bracklesham Cl
Totland Cl
Hawley Lane
The Sixth Form College
ROAD
Mariners Dr
Cem.
Surrey County
Hampshire County
Aldwick Cl
Whitehouse Close
Prospect Avenue
Baird Road
Bell Cl
Faraday Rd
Newton Rd
Ship Lane
Woodland Crs
Cherry Wood Primary School
Ballantyne Rd
Austen Rd
Fleming Cl
Grenville Gdns
Cross Farm Infant School
Farnborough North Station
St Michael's Rd
Burnsall Cl
Sherington Cl
Henry Tyndale School
Works
Farnborough RFC
Napoleon Av
Revelstoke Avenue
Vesey Cl
Prospect Rd
Woodstocks
The Chase
Chapel St
Farnborough St
Farnborough Hill School
32
Tile Barn Cl
Empress Av
Pierrefondes Avenue
FARNBOROUGH
Farnborough Green
North Farnborough County Infant School
Leopold Av
Chestnut Road
Squirrel La
Douglas Pl
Lane
Chingford Avenue
Rectory Road
Highgate
A325
Queen Elizabeth Park
Farnborough Street
Cabrol Road
Farnborough Main Station
On Va Ct
St Michaels Abbey
Brewers
Stake La
Jubilee Hall Rd
Union Street
Priory St
Works
Stourhead Cl
Prospect Road
Holly Cl
Greens School La
High Vw Cl
Windsor Cl
Station Rd
Elm Gv Rd
Clockhouse Road
Sarah Wy
Surgery
Abbey Way
Monks Cl
Douai Cl
Road
Barnes Cl
Ashley Road
Woburn Avenue
VICTORIA RD
Kingsmead
FARNBOROUGH ROAD
Rectory Road
The Garth
Ashley Rd
Primary School
Brookwood
Orchard Rd
B3014
COVE RD
Windsor Close
Nmd
Queensmead
Salisbury
Carlyon Cl
Junior School
Gd Ct
Superstore
Marrowbrook Cl
Princes Mead Shopping Centre
42
Tregolls Dr
Farnborough Park
Manor Road
Hinstock Cl
Works
Market
Superstore
Oak Rd
The Crescent
Wymering Ct
Blaise Cl
Avenue
Wilton Ct
Charlecote Cl
FARNBOROUGH
Westmead
Recreation Centre
Police Station
Farnborough Road
Avenue
Waverley Rd
The Sycamores
Cedar Road
Cedar Rd
Kingsgrove Ind Est
A331

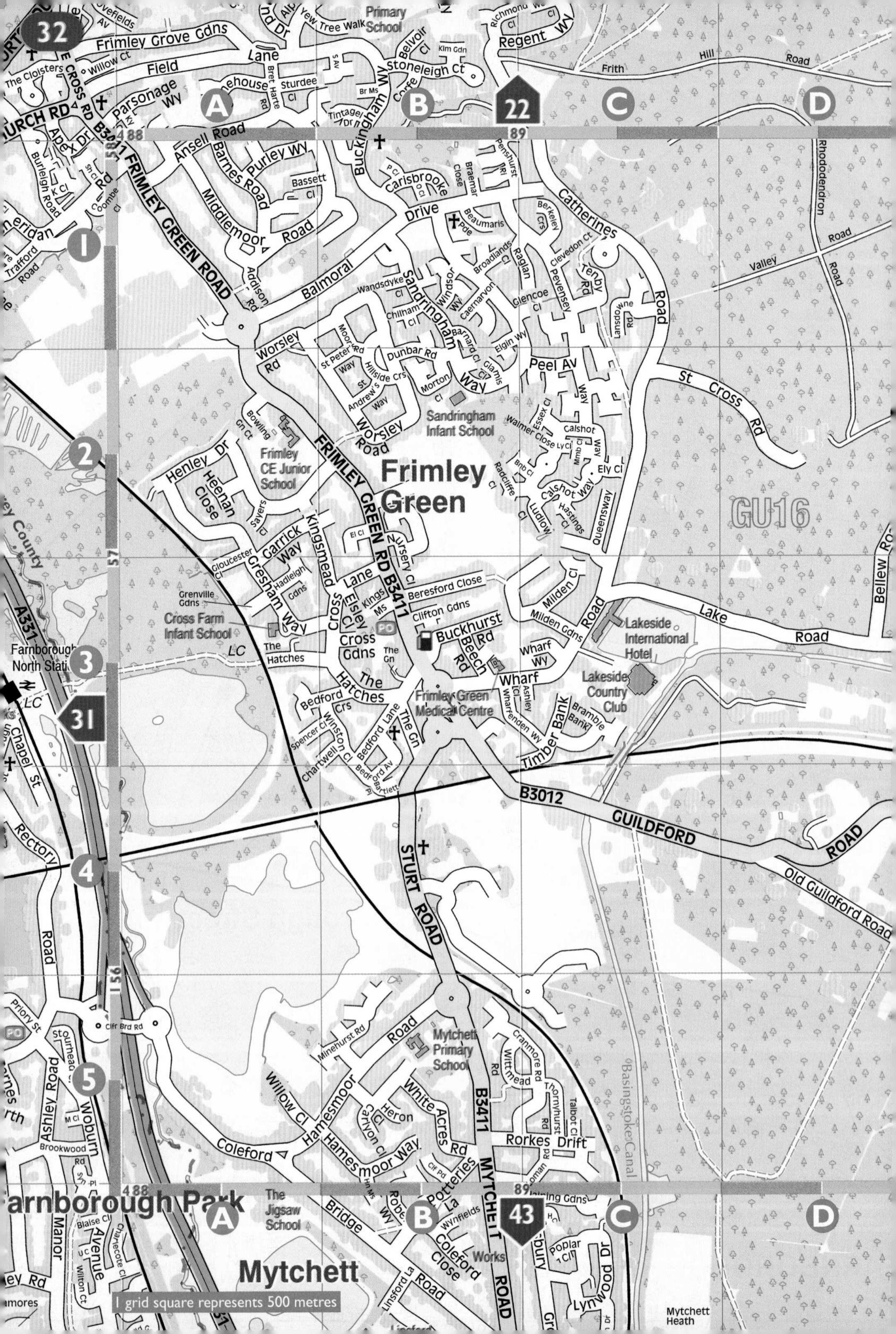

32
22
31
43
Frimley Green
Mytchett
Farnborough Park
Frimley Grove Gdns
Field
Lane
Parsonage Wy
Ansell Road
Frimley Green Road
Balmoral
Drive
Worsley Rd
Worsley Road
Sandringham Way
Catherines Road
St Cross Rd
Lake Road
Rhododendron Road
Valley Road
Frith Hill Road
Regent Wy
Stoneleigh Ct
Buckingham Wy
Middlemoor Road
Barnes Road
Purley Wy
Henley Dr
Heenan Close
Garrick Way
Gresham Way
Kingsmead
Cross Lane
Frimley Green Rd B3411
Beresford Close
Clifton Gdns
Buckhurst Rd
Beech Rd
Wharf Wy
Wharf
Timber Bank
Milden Cl
Milden Gdns
Peel Av
Queensway
Calshot Way
Sandringham Infant School
Frimley CE Junior School
Cross Farm Infant School
Frimley Green Medical Centre
Lakeside International Hotel
Lakeside Country Club
The Hatches
Bedford Crs
Bedford Lane
The Gn
B3012
Guildford Road
Old Guildford Road
Sturt Road
Mytchett Road
B3411
Mytchett Primary School
Hamesmoor Way
Coleford
Willow Cl
White Acres Rd
Rorkes Drift
Basingstoke Canal
A331
Farnborough North Station
Rectory
Chapel St
Ashley Road
Woburn
Manor
Avenue
Bridge
Coleford Close
Road
The Jigsaw School
Works
Lynwood Dr
Mytchett Heath
GU16
LC
488
89
57
56
1 grid square represents 500 metres

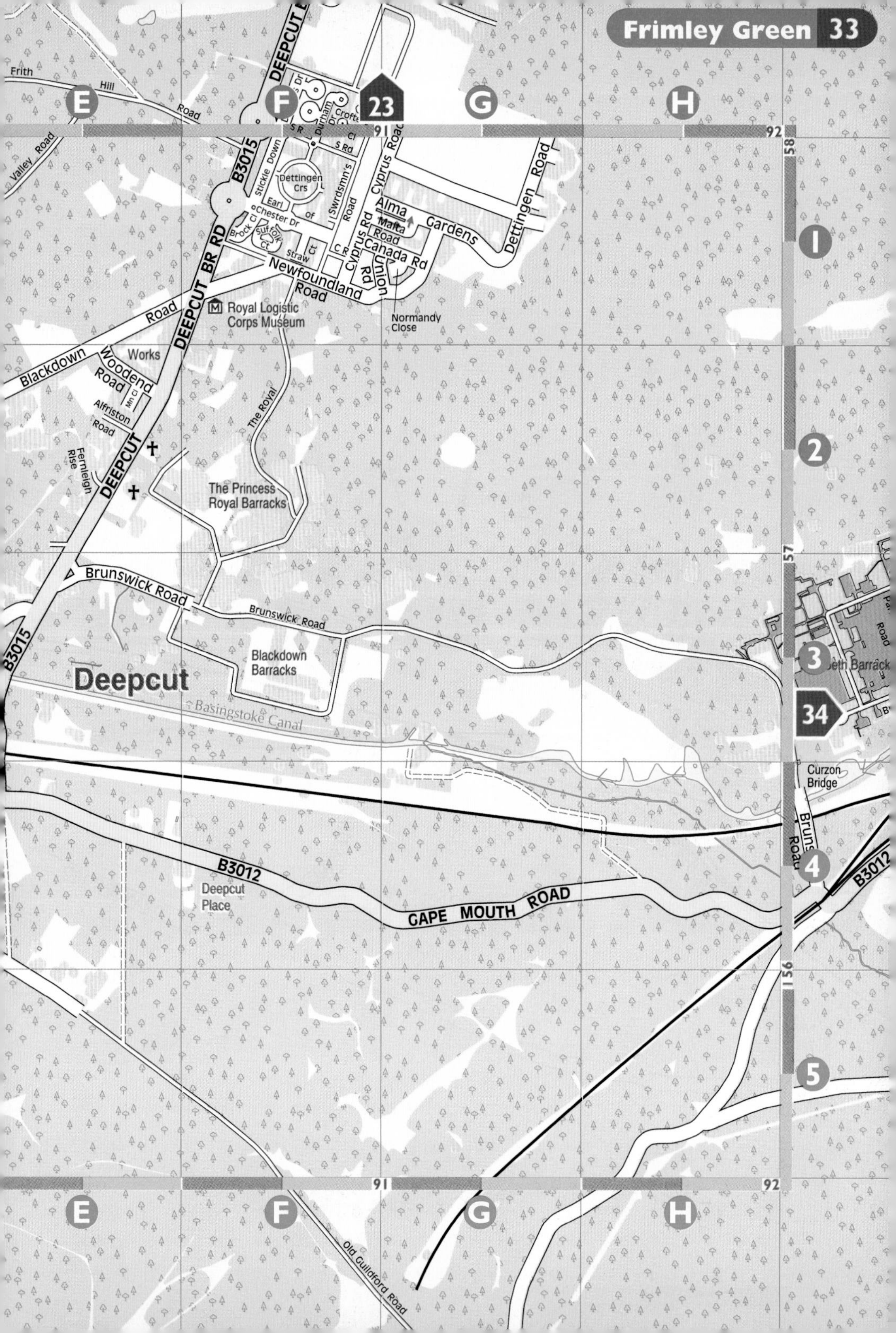
Frith Hill Road
Valley Road
DEEPCUT BR RD
B3015
Stickle Down
Dettingen Crs
Earl of Chester Dr
Brock Cl
Suffolk Ct
Straw Ct
Swrdsmn's Road
Durham Dr
Crofts Cl
S Rd
Cyprus Road
Cyprus Rd
Dettingen Road
Alma Gardens
Malta Road
Canada Rd
Union Rd
Newfoundland Road
Normandy Close
Royal Logistic Corps Museum
Blackdown Road
Woodend Road
Works
Alfriston Road
Fernleigh Rise
DEEPCUT
The Royal
The Princess Royal Barracks
Brunswick Road
Blackdown Barracks
Deepcut
Basingstoke Canal
B3012
Deepcut Place
GAPE MOUTH ROAD
Curzon Bridge
Brunswick Road
Old Guildford Road
23
34
E F G H
1 2 3 4 5
91 92
58 57 56

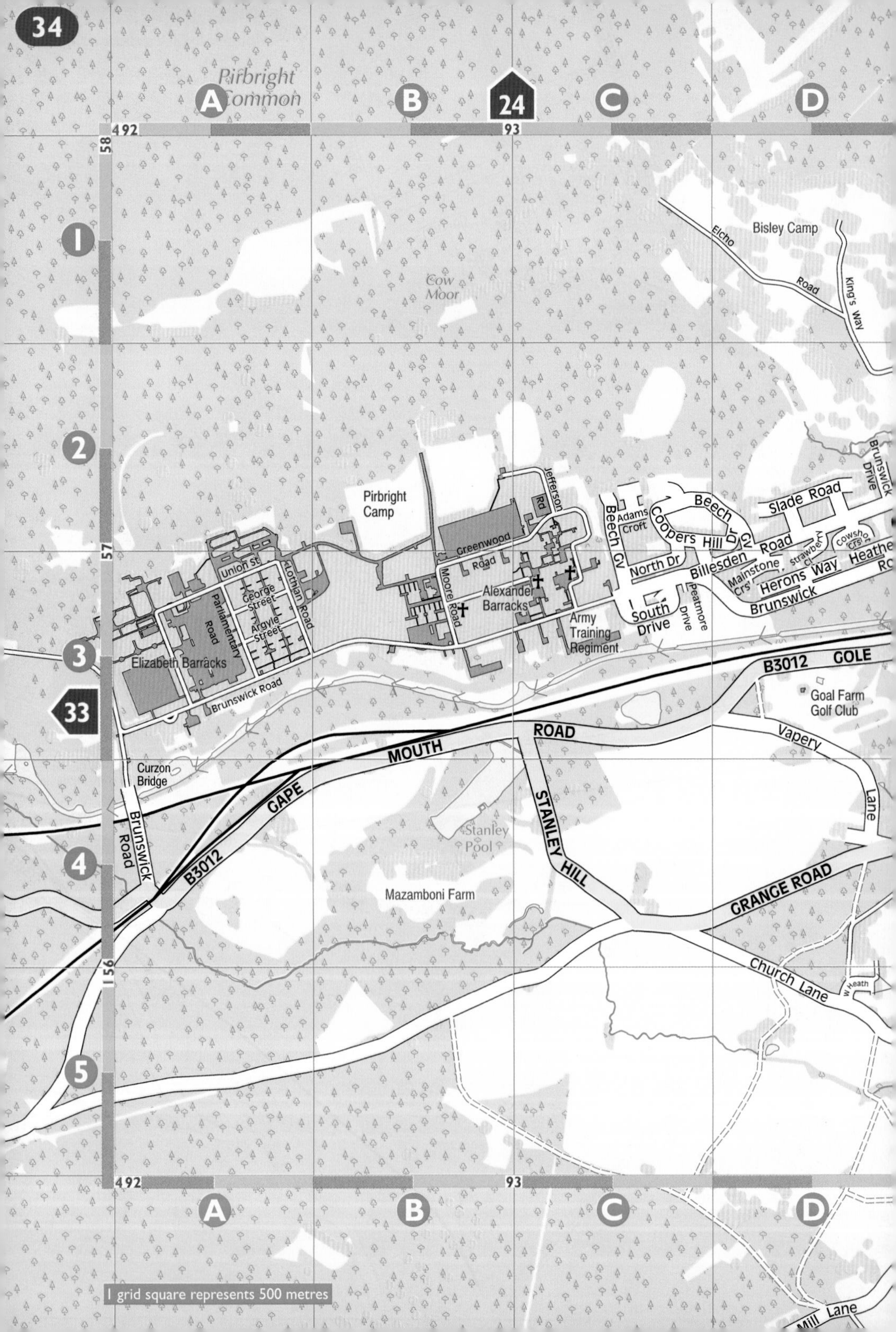
Pirbright Common
A
B
24
C
D
492
93
58
57
56
1
2
3
4
5
33
Bisley Camp
Elcho Road
King's Way
Cow Moor
Brunswick Drive
Slade Road
Beech Cl
Coopers Hill Dr
Adams Croft
Beech Gv
Jefferson Rd
Pirbright Camp
Greenwood Road
Union St
Lothian Road
George Street
Argyle Street
Parliamentary Road
Moore Road
Alexander Barracks
North Dr
Billesden Road
Mainstone Crs
Strawberry Cl
Cowshot Crs
Herons Way
Heather
Brunswick Rd
South Drive
Peatmore Drive
Army Training Regiment
Elizabeth Barracks
Brunswick Road
B3012
GOLE
Goal Farm Golf Club
Vapery Lane
ROAD
MOUTH
GAPE
Curzon Bridge
Brunswick Road
STANLEY HILL
Stanley Pool
Mazamboni Farm
GRANGE ROAD
Church Lane
W Heath
Mill Lane
1 grid square represents 500 metres

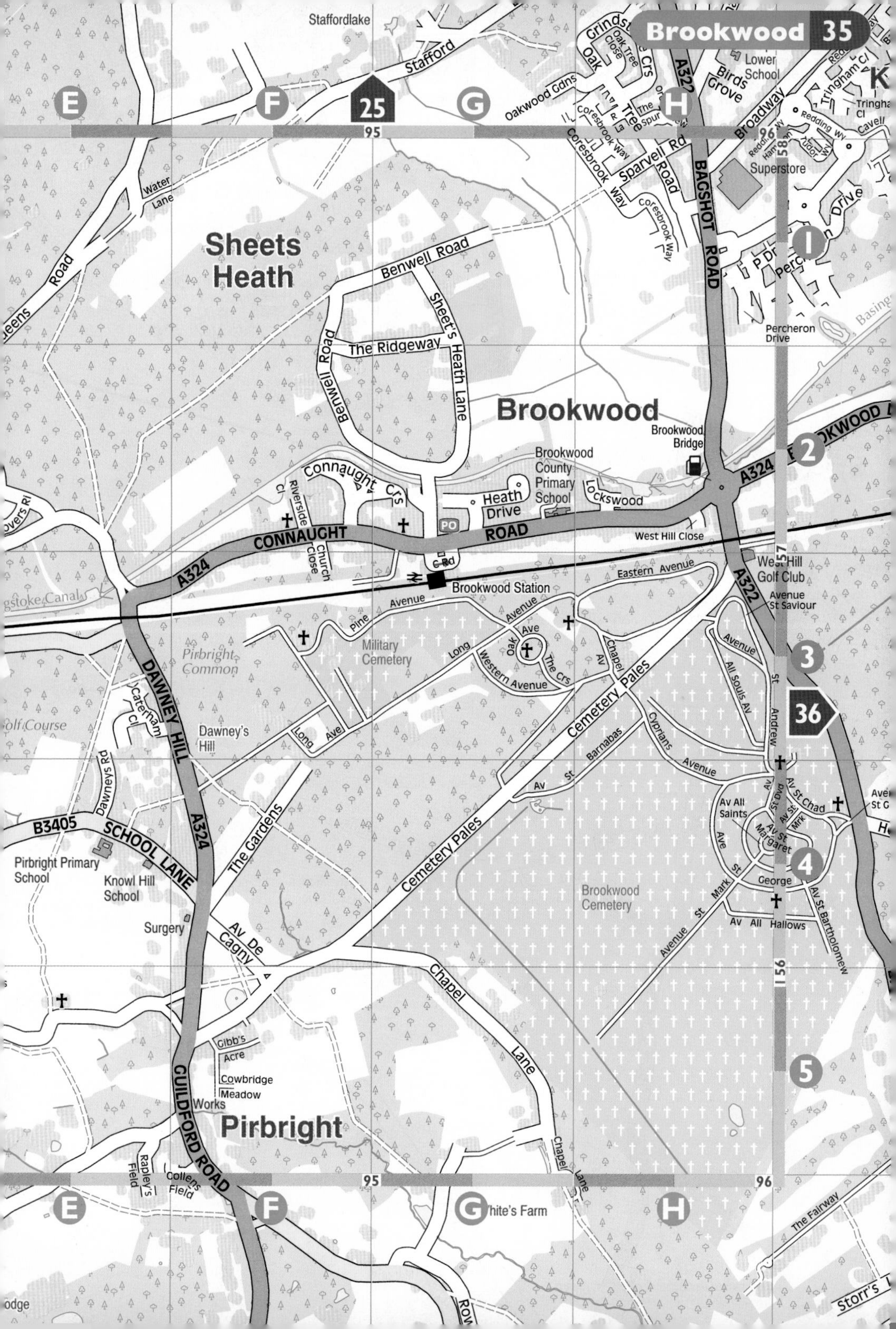
Staffordlake
Stafford
25
E
F
G
H
I
95
96
Water Lane
Queens Road
Sheets Heath
Benwell Road
Sheet's Heath Lane
The Ridgeway
Oakwood Gdns
Oak Tree Close
Coresbrook Way
Sparvell Rd
The Spur
Bagshot Road
A322
Birds Grove
Lower School
Broadway
Superstore
Redding Wy
Tringham Cl
Percheron Drive
Brookwood
Brookwood Bridge
Brookwood County Primary School
Lockswood
Heath Drive
Connaught Crs
Riverside Cl
Church Close
Connaught Road
A324
PO
West Hill Close
West Hill Golf Club
Brookwood Station
Eastern Avenue
Pine Avenue
Long Avenue
Oak Ave
The Crs
Western Avenue
Chapel Av
Military Cemetery
Avenue St Saviour
All Souls Av
St Andrew
Cemetery Pales
Cyprians Avenue
Av St Barnabas
Av St Chad
Av All Saints
Av St Margaret
St George
Av St Mark
Avenue St Mark
Av All Hallows
Av St Bartholomew
Brookwood Cemetery
2
3
4
5
36
Pirbright Common
Dawney Hill
Dawney's Hill
Caterham Cl
Dawneys Rd
B3405
School Lane
Pirbright Primary School
Knowl Hill School
Surgery
The Gardens
Av De Cagny
Chapel Lane
Gibb's Acre
Cowbridge Meadow
Works
Pirbright
Guildford Road
Rapley's Field
Collens Field
White's Farm
The Fairway
Storr's
Golf Course
Basingstoke Canal
157
156

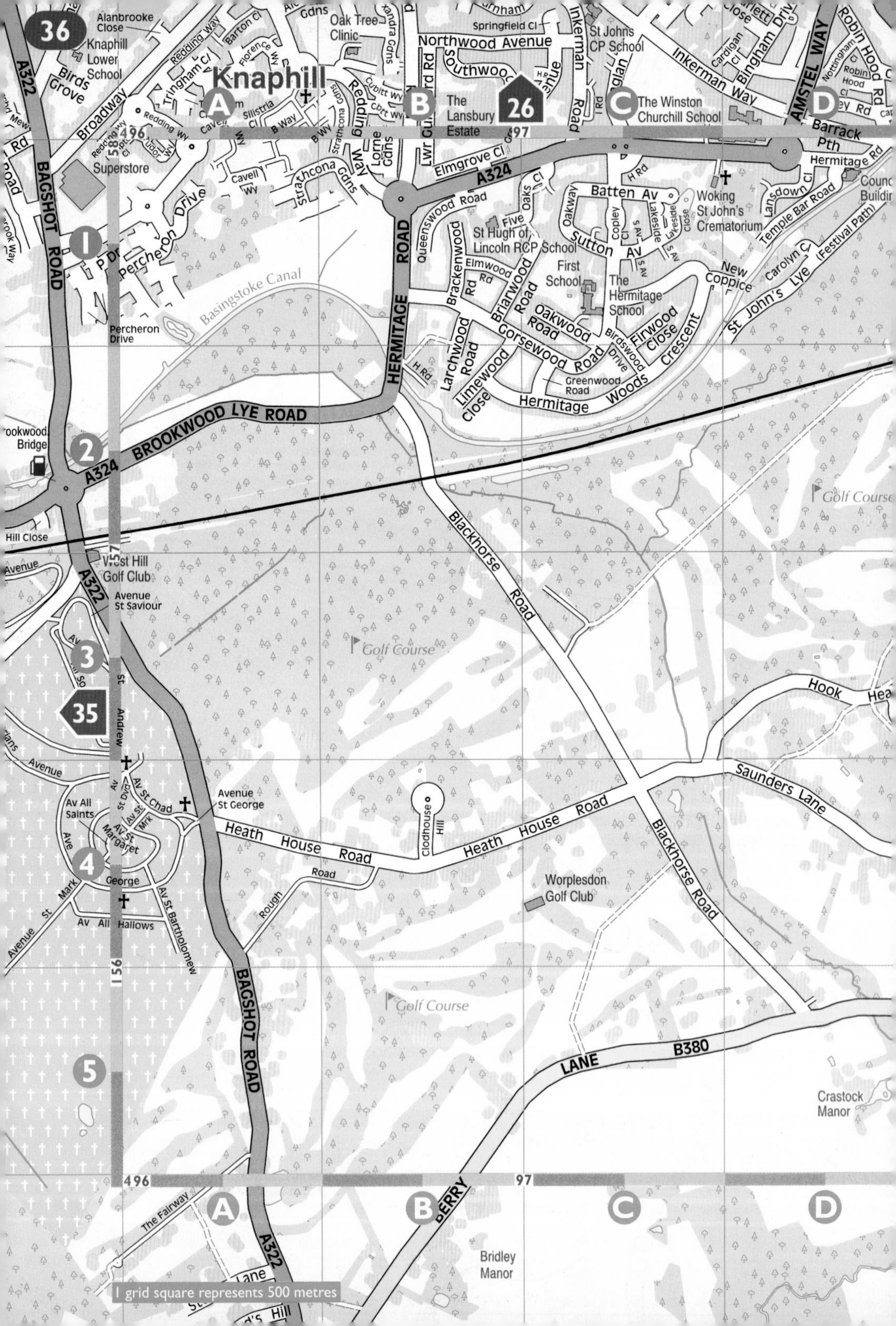

36
Knaphill
Alanbrooke Close
Knaphill Lower School
Birds Grove
Broadway
Superstore
Percheron Drive
Basingstoke Canal
Hermitage Road
The Lansbury Estate
26
Northwood Avenue
Oak Tree Clinic
St Johns CP School
Inkerman Way
The Winston Churchill School
Amstel Way
Barrack Pth
Hermitage Rd
Elmgrove Cl
A324
Queenswood Road
St Hugh of Lincoln RCP School
Batten Av
Sutton Av
First School
The Hermitage School
Woking St John's Crematorium
Temple Bar Road
St John's Lye (Festival Path)
New Coppice
Brackenwood Rd
Briarwood Road
Elmwood Rd
Oakwood Road
Gorsewood Road
Larchwood Road
Limewood Close
Firwood Close
Birdswood Drive
Hermitage Woods Crescent
Greenwood Road
Brookwood Lye Road
Brookwood Bridge
Bagshot Road
A322
West Hill Golf Club
Avenue St Saviour
35
Golf Course
Blackhorse Road
Hook Heath
Saunders Lane
Avenue St George
Heath House Road
Clodhouse Hill
Rough Road
Worplesdon Golf Club
Av St Chad
Av All Saints
Av St Margaret
Av All Hallows
Av St Bartholomew
Avenue St Mark
St Andrew
Lane B380
Berry
Crastock Manor
Bridley Manor
The Fairway
496
97
157
156
1 grid square represents 500 metres

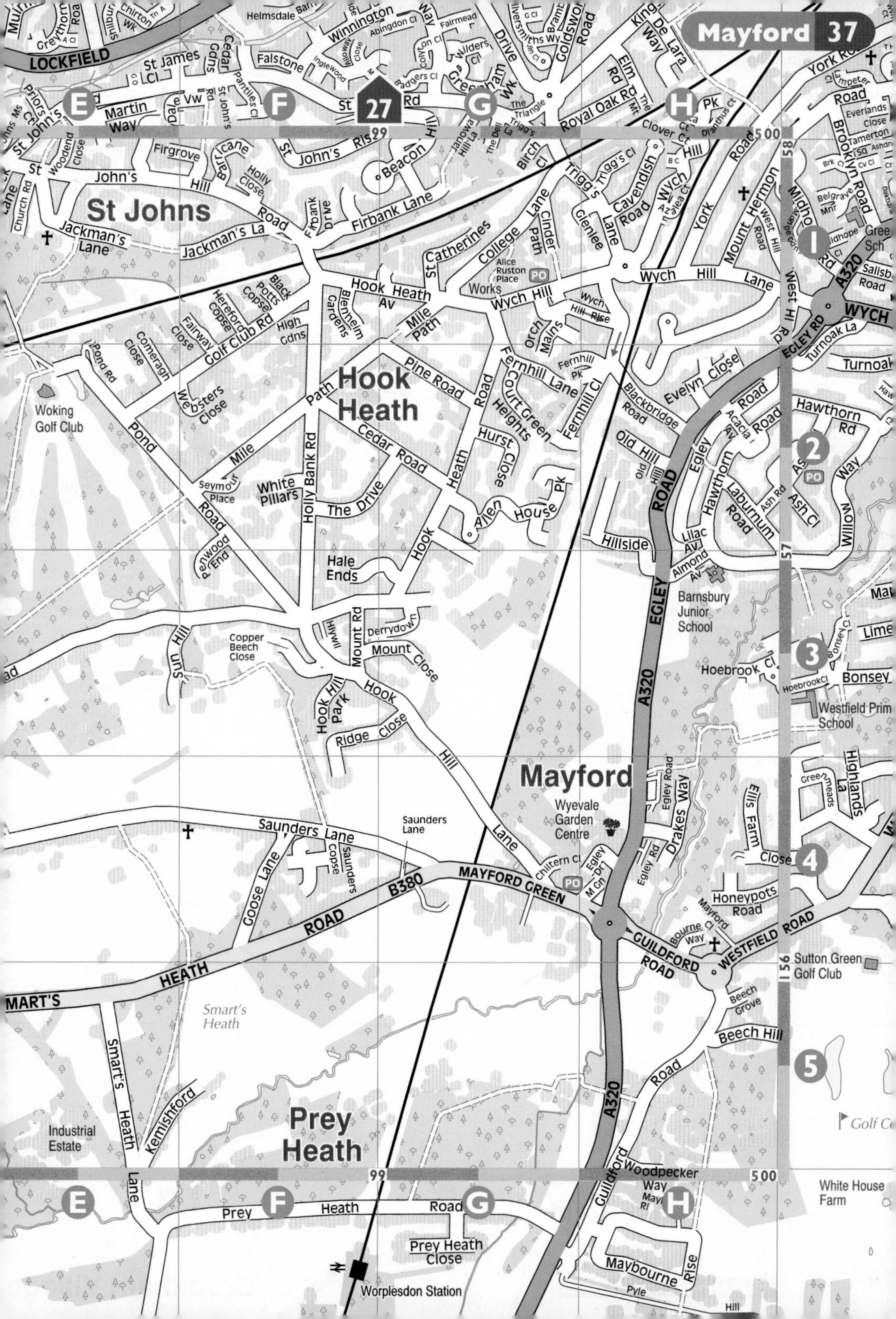
St Johns
Hook Heath
Mayford
Prey Heath
Woking Golf Club
Barnsbury Junior School
Westfield Primary School
Wyevale Garden Centre
Sutton Green Golf Club
Worplesdon Station
Smart's Heath
Industrial Estate
White House Farm
Lockfield
St John's Hill Road
Jackman's Lane
Hook Heath Road
Hook Heath Av
Pond Road
Mile Path
Golf Club Rd
Cedar Road
Pine Road
Holly Bank Rd
The Drive
Hook Hill
Saunders Lane
Mayford Green
Smart's Heath Road
Egley Road
Guildford Road
Westfield Road
Wych Hill Lane
York Road
Mount Hermon Road
Goose Lane
Prey Heath Road
Prey Heath Close
Maybourne Rise
Woodpecker Way
Hawthorn Rd
Laburnum Road
Beech Hill
Beech Grove
Honeypots Road
Ellis Farm Close
Drakes Way
Bonsey Lane
Hoebrook Cl
Evelyn Close
Blackbridge Road
Old Hill
Hillside
Fernhill Lane
Allen House Pk
Hurst Close
Ridge Close
Mount Close
Hale Ends
White Pillars
Seymour Place
Penwood End
Webster Close
Firbank Lane
Beacon Hill
Kemishford
A320
B380

Days Inn Hotel
Kingsley Sq
Kingsworthy Rd
Lasham Rd
Mounts Way
Lower Mount Street
Ramsdell Rd
Turners Way
Knights Enham Dr
Hursley Dr
Hawkley Wy
Elvetham Heath Prim Sch
Palelane Farm
Mounts Way
Comm Cen
The Key
Superstore
Elvetham Heath Way
Alfred Cl
Chawton Cl
Chineham Cl
Elvetham Heath Way
Elvetham Crs
Elvetham Road
West Hl Gdns
READING ROAD NORTH
Glendale Pk
Broomrigg Road
Fitzroy Road
Pale Lane
Perry Dr
Dukes
The Oaks
Mead
Priory Cl
Tavistock
Woodcote Gn
Calthorpe Park School
Tavistock Rd
Road
Hart Sports Centre
Tavistock Infant School
All Saints CE Junior School
The Hurst
Barley Mow Close
Hitches Lane
New Barn
Larmer Cl
Swan Way
Dogmersfield CE Primary School
Dogmersfield
Pilcot
Road
Crookham Village
44
A
B
C
D
1
2
3
4
5
478
79
55
54
53

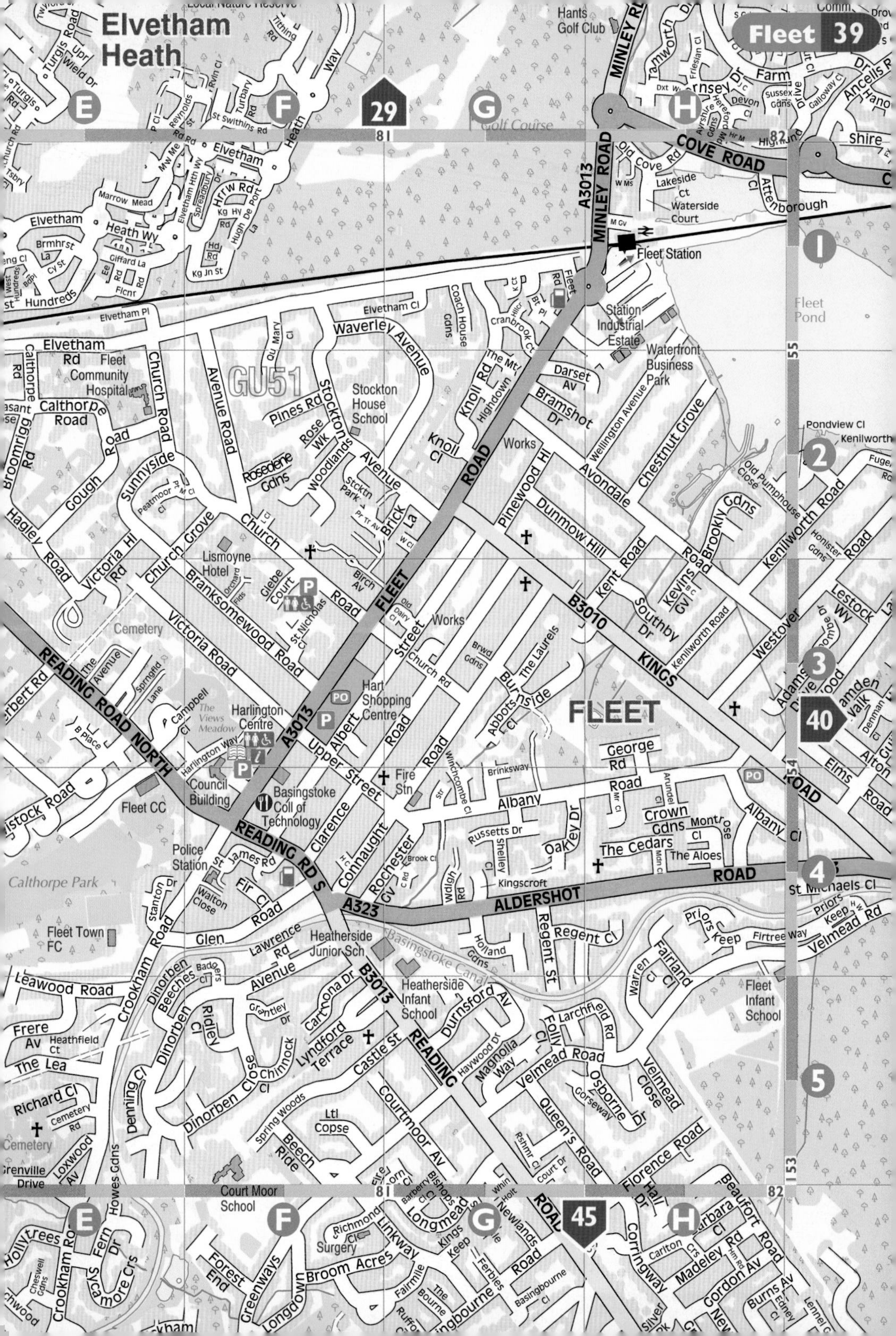
Elvetham Heath
Hants Golf Club
Golf Course
MINLEY ROAD
A3013
COVE ROAD
Old Cove Rd
Lakeside Ct
Waterside Court
Attenborough
Fleet Station
Fleet Pond
Station Industrial Estate
Waterfront Business Park
Elvetham Pl
Elvetham Cl
Elvetham Rd
Fleet Community Hospital
Calthorpe Road
Church Road
Avenue Road
GU51
Waverley Avenue
Stockton Avenue
Stockton House School
Pines Rd
Rose Wk
Woodlands
Rosedene Gdns
Coach House Gdns
Cranbrook Ct
The Mt
Knoll Rd
Knoll Cl
Highdown
Darset Av
Bramshot Dr
Wellington Avenue
Chestnut Grove
Works
Pinewood Hl
Dunmow Hill
Avondale
Avondale Road
Brookly Gdns
Old Pumphouse Close
Kenilworth Road
Pondview Cl
Kenilworth
Westover
Kent Road
Kevins Gv
Southby Dr
B3010
KINGS ROAD
FLEET
Gough Road
Hagley Road
Victoria Hl Rd
Sunnyside
Church Grove
Lismoyne Hotel
Branksomewood Road
Glebe Court
St Nicholas Cl
Church Road
Victoria Road
Cemetery
Birch Av
Brick La
FLEET ROAD
Old Dairy Cl
Albert Street
Church Rd
Brwd Gdns
The Laurels
Burnside
Abbots Cl
Hart Shopping Centre
Upper Street
Albert Road
Road
READING ROAD NORTH
The Avenue
Springfld Lane
Campbell Cl
The Views Meadow
Harlington Centre
Harlington Way
Council Building
Basingstoke Coll of Technology
Fleet CC
Fire Stn
Winchcombe Cl
Brinksway
George Rd
Albany Road
Crown Gdns
Montrose Cl
The Cedars
The Aloes
Albany Cl
Russetts Dr
Oakley Dr
Shelley Cl
Kingscroft
ALDERSHOT ROAD
A323
St Michaels Cl
Priors Keep
Firtree Way
Velmead Rd
Calthorpe Park
Police Station
St James Rd
Fir Cl
READING RD S
Clarence Road
Connaught Road
Rochester Gv
Brook Cl
Walton Close
Stanton Dr
Glen Road
Fleet Town FC
Lawrence Rd
Lawrence Avenue
Heatherside Junior Sch
Basingstoke Canal
Holland Gdns
Regent St
Regent Cl
Warren Cl
Fairland Cl
Fleet Infant School
Leawood Road
Crookham Road
Dinorben Beeches
Badgers Cl
Ridley Cl
Grantley Dr
B3013
Heatherside Infant School
Durnsford Av
Larchfield Rd
Folly Cl
Frere Av
Heathfield Ct
The Lea
Dinorben
Dinorben Close
Chinnock Cl
Carmona Dr
Lyndford Terrace
Castle St
READING ROAD
Haywood Dr
Magnolia Way
Velmead Road
Velmead Close
Osborne Dr
Gorseway
Richard Cl
Cemetery Rd
Cemetery
Denning Cl
Spring Woods
Beech Ride
Ltl Copse
Courtmoor Av
Queen's Road
Court Dr
Florence Road
Grenville Drive
Loxwood Av
Howes Gdns
Court Moor School
Bishops Cl
Longmead
Newlands Road
Hall Dr
Beaufort Road
Barbara Cl
Hollytrees
Crookham Rd
Fern Dr
Sycamore Crs
Forest End
Greenways
Richmond Cl
Surgery
Broom Acres
Linkway
Kings Keep
Longdown
Fairmile
The Bourne
Ferbies
Basingbourne Road
Basingbourne Cl
Corringway
Carlton Crs
Madeley Rd
Gordon Av
Burns Av
Edney
Lennel Cl

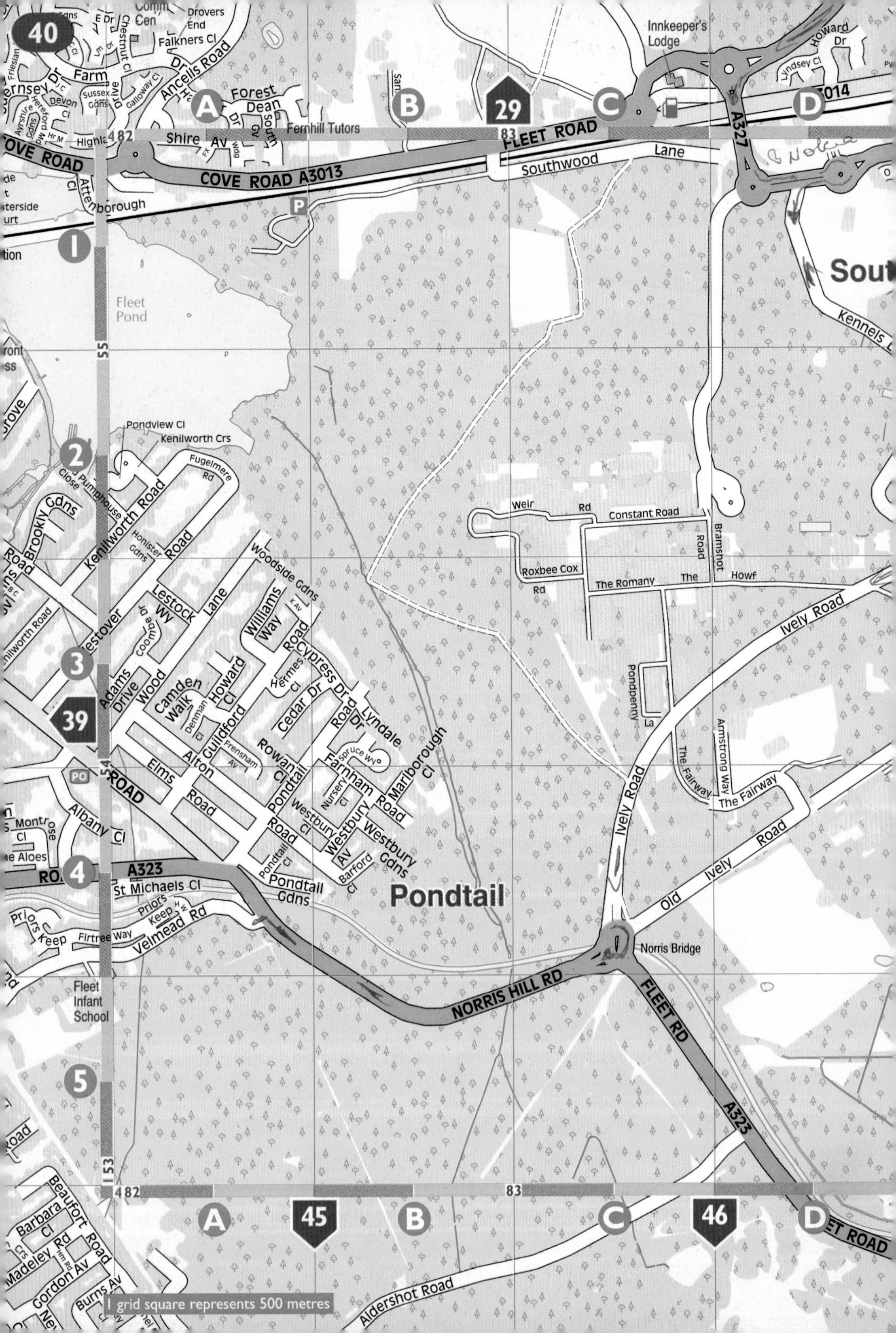
Innkeeper's Lodge
Drovers End
Falkners Cl
Ancells Road
Forest Dean
Farm
Fernhill Tutors
FLEET ROAD
COVE ROAD
COVE ROAD A3013
Southwood Lane
Attenborough
A327
Howard Dr
Lindsey Cl
Fleet Pond
Kennels
Pondview Cl
Kenilworth Crs
Fugelmere Rd
Pumphouse Close
Brookly Gdns
Kenilworth Road
Honister Gdns
Road
Woodside Gdns
Lestock Wy
Lane
Williams Way
Westover
Coombe Dr
Cypress Dr
Hermes Cl
Adams Drive
Wood
Camden Walk
Howard Cl
Denman Cl
Guildford
Cedar Dr
Lyndale Dr
Road
Spruce Wy
Frensham Av
Rowan Cl
Marlborough Cl
Alton
Elms Road
Road
Pondtail
Farnham Road
Nursery Cl
Westbury Cl
Westbury Av
Westbury Gdns
Pondtail Cl
Barford Cl
Pondtail Gdns
Pondtail
Albany Cl
Montrose Cl
ROAD
A323
St Michaels Cl
Priors Keep
Firtree Way
Velmead Rd
Fleet Infant School
NORRIS HILL RD
FLEET RD
A323
Norris Bridge
Weir Rd
Constant Road
Bramshot Road
Roxbee Cox Rd
The Romany
The Howf
Ively Road
Pondpenny La
Armstrong Way
The Fairway
Old Ively Road
Ively Road
Beaufort Road
Barbara Cl
Madeley Rd
Gordon Av
Burns Av
Aldershot Road
ET ROAD
Road
1 grid square represents 500 metres

29
39
45
46

Rindle Cl
Chiltern Cl
Chiltern Avenue
Jubilee Close
Apollo Rise
Armstrong Mall
Columbus Dr
Aldrin
Southwood Road
Morval
Buttermere Cl
Surgery
Cove CC
COVE ROAD
Nash
BRIDGE RD
Highfield
Elmsleigh Rd
Sheffield Cl
Welbeck Cl
Avenue
B3014
Gables Cl
Marrowbrook Cl
Tower Hl
SUMMIT AVENUE
Summit Av
Gleneagles Dr
Larch Way
Long Beech Dr
Superstore
Surgery
Southwood Infant Sch
Laurel Cl
Links Way
New Dawn Cl
Briars Cl
Griffon Cl
Merlin Way
Maskell Wy
Fox Heath
Randolph Dr
Southwood
Delville Cl
Mc Naughton Cl
Crerar Cl
The Copse
Broadmead
Lane
Richmond Cl
Rose Gdns
Alpine Cl
The Rockery
The Lawns
The Shrubbery
Southern Way
The Topiary
Garden Cl
Wisley Gdns
Tarn Cl
IVELY RD
Ively Road
IVELY ROAD
Ambleside Cl
Ullswater Av
Grasmere Rd
Coniston
Rafborough
Premier Inn
Golf Course
Southwood Golf Club
Hazel Avenue
Dene Rd
Brookhouse Road
Cody Road
Beverley Crs
Brook Gardens
Kempton Ct
Arrow Road
Arrow Industrial Est
Eelmoor Rd
Montgomery Rd
Hunter Rd
Murray Rd
Halifax Cl
Alison Cl
Primary School
Fowler Rd
Busk Crs
Goodden Crs
Keith Lucas Rd
Marrowbrook
Invincible Road
St Christopher's Road
Weir Av
Weir Cl
Lane
FARNE
ELLES ROAD A327
Farnborough Business Centre
Eelmoor Road Depot
Trading Est
Fowler Av
Templer Av
Perring Rd
Meadow Ga Av
Wessex Rd
Mosquito Way
Range Rd
Ively Road
Kennels Lane
Donlan Dr
Old Ively Rd
Range Road
Ce Rd
Whitley Way
Dump Rd
Rocket Rd
Reservoir Rd
Brake Rd
Tunnel Rd
Cross Rd
Radar Road
Romney Rd
Link Road
Warwick Rd
Magazine Rd
Valiant Way
Wigan Rd
Wellesley Rd
Windsor Rd
Walrus Rd
Diamond Way
Vampire Way
Wapiti Way
Victor Way
Buccaneer Way
York Road
Farnborough Airport
Camel Way
Dingley Way
Hinaldi
Gulley Rd
Beaufighter Rd
Canberra Way
AeroPark Business Park
Devon
Farnborough Aerospace Centre
Gladiator Way
Aerospace Bld
Arspc Bvd
Hurricane Way
Halifax Way
Swordfish Way
Spitfire
Seafire Wy
Business Aviation Centre
Woodside Rd
Wellington Way
Stirling Way
Berkshire
Copse Rd
Sidestrand Rd
Devon Road
Barracuda Rd
Victoria Track
Watts Common
Track
Gate Road
Pavilion
Laffan
Laffan's Rd
Laffan Track
Eelmoor Bridge
SBAC
Army Golf Club
Watts Common
Golf Course
Shoe Lane
30
42
47

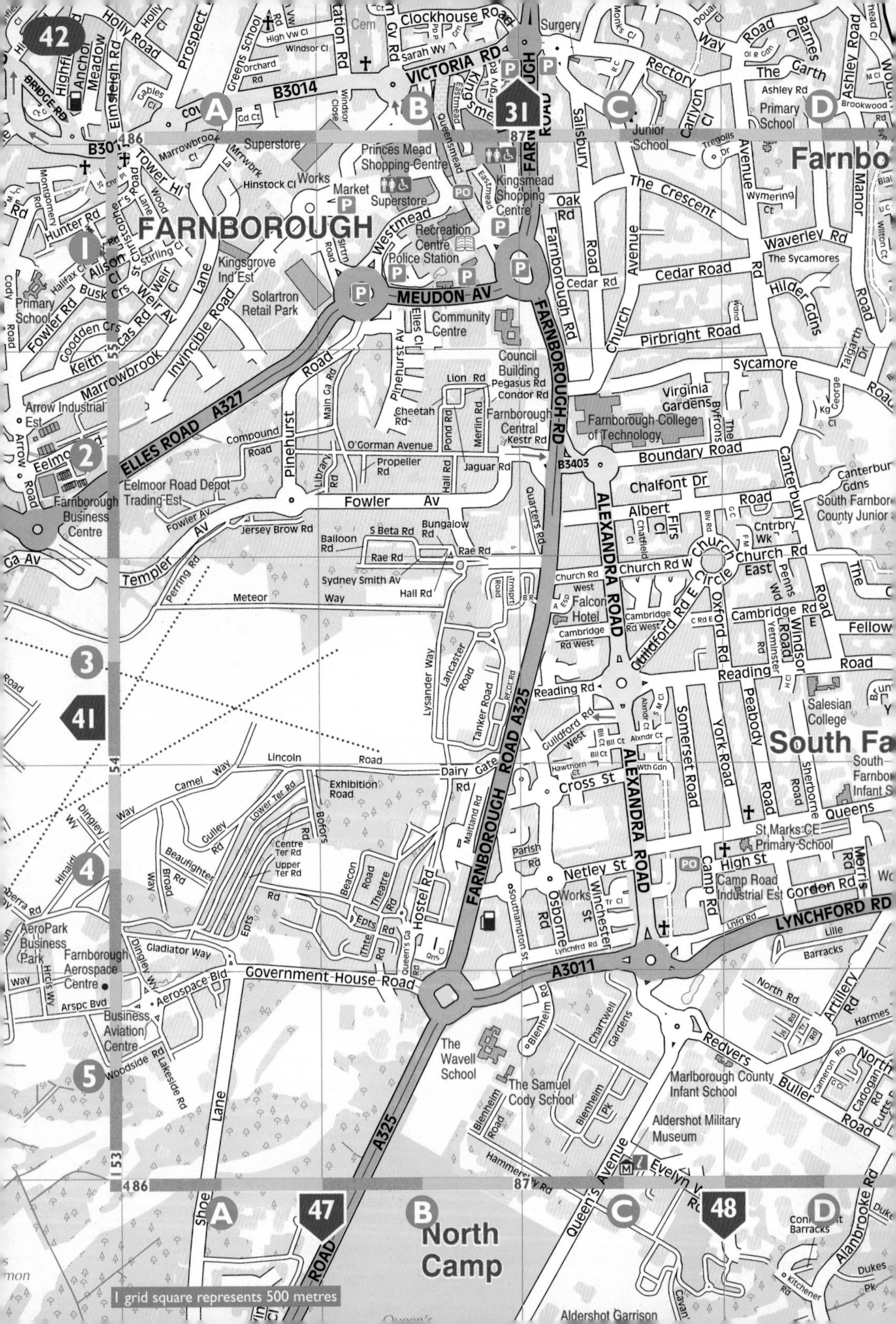

42
FARNBOROUGH
Farnbo
South Fa
North Camp
Aldershot Garrison
A
B
C
D
1
2
3
4
5
31
41
47
48
486
487
486
487
55
54
53
1 grid square represents 500 metres
Clockhouse Road
VICTORIA RD
B3014
Rectory
Road
Barnes Cl
Ashley Road
The Garth
Ashley Rd
Primary School
Brookwood
Junior School
Farnborough Road
Salisbury
Carlyon Cl
Surgery
Highfield
Anchor
Meadow
Elmsleigh Rd
Holly Road
Prospect
Greens School
High Vw Cl
Windsor Cl
Orchard Rd
Sarah Wy
Gables Cl
Gd Ct
Windsor Close
Eastmead
Queensmead
Kingsmead
BRIDGE RD
Superstore
Princes Mead Shopping Centre
Works
Market
Superstore
Kingsmead Shopping Centre
Tower Hl
Marrowbrook Cl
Hinstock Cl
Oak Rd
The Crescent
Avenue
Wymering Ct
Tregolls Dr
Montgomery Rd
Hunter Rd
St Christopher's Road
Lane
Wood
Westmead
Recreation Centre
Police Station
Kingsgrove Ind Est
Solartron Retail Park
Stirling Cl
Alison Cl
Busk Crs
Weir Av
Weir
Halifax Cl
Primary School
Fowler Rd
Goodden Crs
Keith Lucas Rd
Invincible Road
Marrowbrook
MEUDON AV
Elles Cl
Pinehurst Av
Community Centre
Council Building
Lion Rd
Pegasus Rd
Condor Rd
Cheetah Rd
Pond Rd
Merlin Rd
Farnborough Central
Kestr Rd
FARNBOROUGH RD
Cedar Rd
Church
Avenue
Cedar Road
Waverley Rd
The Sycamores
Hilder Gdns
Pirbright Road
Sycamore
Road
Talgarth Dr
Manor
Virginia Gardens
Byfrons
The
Farnborough College of Technology
Arrow Industrial Est
ELLES ROAD A327
Eelmoor Rd
Arrow Road
Compound Road
Pinehurst
Main Ga Rd
O'Gorman Avenue
Library Rd
Propeller Rd
Hall Rd
Jaguar Rd
B3403
Boundary Road
Canterbury
Canterbury Gdns
South Farnborough County Junior
Eelmoor Road Depot Trading Est
Farnborough Business Centre
Fowler Av
Fowler Av
Jersey Brow Rd
Balloon Rd
S Beta Rd
Bungalow Rd
Rae Rd
Rae Rd
Sydney Smith Av
Hall Rd
Quarters Rd
Chalfont Dr
ALEXANDRA ROAD
Albert Cl
Firs
Chatfield Cl
Cntrbry Wk
Church Circle
Church Rd
East
Church Rd W
Templer Av
Perring Rd
Meteor Way
Church Rd West
Falcon Hotel
Cambridge Rd West
Cambridge Rd West
Guildford Rd E
Oxford Rd
Penns Wd
Road
Cambridge Rd
Windsor Road
Fellow
Yetminster Rd
Reading Road
Reading Rd
Lysander Way
Lancaster Road
Tanker Road
FARNBOROUGH ROAD A325
Guildford Rd West
Somerset Road
York Road
Peabody Road
Salesian College
Lincoln Road
Dairy Gate Rd
Camel Way
Exhibition Road
Lower Ter Rd
Hawthorn Ct
Wth Gdn
Cross St
ALEXANDRA ROAD
Sherborne Road
South Farnborough Infant S
Queens
Dingley Wy
Way
Gulley Rd
Centre Ter Rd
Upper Ter Rd
Bofors Rd
Maitland Rd
Parish Rd
St Marks CE Primary School
Beaufighter
Broad Rd
Way
Beacon Road
Theatre Rd
Hostel Rd
Netley St
Works
Winchester St
Osborne Rd
Camp Rd
High St
Camp Road Industrial Est
Gordon Rd
Morris Rd
Hinaldi
Canberra Rd
AeroPark Business Park
Farnborough Aerospace Centre
Gladiator Way
Epts
Epts Rd
Thte Rd
Queen's Ga Rd
Southampton St
Lynchfrd Rd
LYNCHFORD RD
Lille Barracks
Dingley Wy
Aerospace Bld
Government House Road
A3011
Arspc Bvd
Business Aviation Centre
Blenheim Rd
Chartwell Gardens
North Rd
Artillery Rd
Harmes
Redvers
Buller
Cameron Rd
Cadogan
North
Cutts
Woodside Rd
Lakeside Rd
The Wavell School
The Samuel Cody School
Blenheim Road
Blenheim Pk
Marlborough County Infant School
Aldershot Military Museum
Road
Lane
A325
Hammersley Rd
Queen's Avenue
Evelyn Av
Shoe
ROAD
Connaught Barracks
Alanbrooke Rd
Dukes
Kitchener Rd

Primary School
Willow Cl
Hamesmoor
Heron
Carlyon Cl
White Acres Rd
B3411
Wittmead
Thornyhurst
Talbot Cl
32
Drift
Basingstoke Canal
E
F
G
H
Coleford
Hamesmoor Wy
Potteries La
MYTCHETT ROAD
89
90
gh Park
The Jigsaw School
Bridge
Robert Wy
Wynfields
Haining Gdns
Salisbury Grove
Poplar Cl
Lynwood Dr
Mytchett
Coleford Close
Works
Linsford La
Road
A331
Linsford Business Park
Mytchett Heath
Salisbury Ter
Mytchett Place Road
B3411
Ambleside Cl
Road
Jubilee
The Gld
Hazel Rd
Glenmount Rd
Grayswood Drive
Mytchett Place
Barnsley Cl
Keogh Close
Saltram Rd
Ashdown Av
Collingwood
Sycamore Rd
Corfe Wy
Cumbria Ct
The Wrekin
Rodmel Ct
Whites Rd
South St
Park
Drake Av
Mytchett Lake Road
Army Medical Services Museum
Keogh Barracks
Mytchett Lake
Mytchett Rd
orough
Meadow Close
STRATFORD RD B3165
FRIMLEY ROAD
Warwick Rd
Salesian View
Lynchford Lane
Carrington La
Holly Lodge Primary School
Homeleigh Crescent
Winter Cl
Rosemary Avenue
Works
Lynchford Rd
LC
North Camp Station
LYSONS AV
Nexus Park
A3011
Hollybush Lane
B3411
Works
Station Vw
Station Ap
Furze Cl
B3166
Cypress Gv
Birch Wy
Enterprise Industrial Est
Ash Vale Station
Chart House Rd
Works
Station Rd East
Sycamore Dr
Greatbottom Flash
Ramillies Cl
Gort Cl
Wellesley Cl
Avondale
Northcote Rd
Kestrel Cl
Horseshoe Lane
Tournai Cl
Mons Cl
Slim Cl
Maple Cl
Wentworth Cl
Wentworth Crs
Vale Rd
Hollybush Lane
Newfield Rd
49
Ash Vale
ROAD
Rowcroft Cl
Pine Cl
Robin Cl
Heathvale Br Rd
Fir Acre Road
Cuthbert Rd
Ash Comm
I
2
3
4
5
55
54
53

44
38
52
Crookham Village
Pilcot Road
Knight Cl
The Crs
Hillside Cl
The Street
PO
Veronica Drive
Stroud Lane
Crondall Road
Hancock's Farm
Bowenhurst La
Finns Industrial Park
Bowenhurst La
Grove Farm
Velmead Community Centre
The Lea
Larmer Cl
Lea Springs
Swan Way
Netherhouse Moor
Richard Cl
Cemetery Rd
Cemetery
Grenville Drive
Loxwood Av
Howes Gdns
Denning Cl
Dinorben Close
Chinnock Cl
Spring Woods
Ltl Copse
Court Moor School
Hawkins Gv
Hollytrees
Cheswell Gdns
Crookham Road
Fern Dr
Sycamore Crs
Beechwood Cl
Netherhouse Moor
Forest End
Greenways
Longdown
Broom Acres
Richmond Cl
Surgery
Wickham Pl
Wickham Road
GU52
Crookham Reach
Coxheath Road
Malthouse Cl
Wickham Cl
Cranford Avenue
Rowan Dl
Grange Rd
Glades
Basingbourne Rd
Parsons
Conifer Close
Heather Dr
The St
Knox Cl
The W
M Vw
Gally Hill Road
Woodland Rise
Rustic Gln
Sylvan Way
Ferndale
Freelands Dr
Coniston Wy
Leger Cl
Rydal Dr
Award Rd
Slvr Brch Cl
Levignen Cl
Camus Cl
Brandon Rd
Decouttere Cl
Silvester Wy
Jessett Drive
Cvsh Gdns
Langley Cl
Cavendish Road
Crookham CE Infant School
Park Pl
Park
Gn Leys
War Mem
Vicarage Gdns
Gally Hill Road
Gables Road
Moreton Close
Aldershot Road
Gondreville Gdns
Londlandes Drive
Twisell Thorne
Rye Cft
Further Vell-Mead
Le Borowe
Danvers
Hop Gdn
Browning Rd
Spn Md
Fnmn Ck
B Cl
Bn Cl
Hunnels Cl
Daphne Dr
Nether Vell-Mead
Water Rede
Barn Meadow Cl
Browning Rd
Rasset Md
R Cl
Bl Pr Ct
Tryplets
Lynams
Maurier Cl
Du
Redfields La
Garden Centre
Humphrey Park
Humphrey Pk
Ewshot Lane
Tennis Club
Watery Lane
Farriers Close
Stillers Farm
Redfields Business Park
St Nicholas School
Redfields
Redfields Lane
Dare's Lane
Ewshot La
Dares Farm
Downsland
Alley
1 grid square represents 500 metres
479
80
53
52
51
A
B
C
D
1
2
3
4
5

Velmead Road
Osborne Dr
Velmead Close
Gorseway
Queen
Magnolia Way
Florence Rd
Hall Dr
Beaufort Road
Barbara Cl
Madeley Rd
Carlton Crs
Corringway
Cedar Wk
Gordon Av
New Rd
Burns Av
Edney Cl
Lennel Gdns
Gravel Rd
Grove
Northfield Rd
Heron Cl
Spencer Cl
Potters Ind.Park
Coxmoor Cl
Aldershot Road
Pine Cl
Grove Rd
Weldon Cl
Sian Cl
Annes Wy
Silver Pk Cl
SOUTH
ROAD
Longmead
Kings Keep
Silverdale
Newlands Road
Ferbies
Basingbourne Road
Basingbourne Cl
The Bourne
Award Road
Andrews Cl
The Briars
Bryanstone Cl
Vivian Cl
Chiltern Cl
Rounton Road
Kenmore Cl
Compton Cl
Compton Rd
Kingfisher Cl
Ryebeck Rd
Elizabeth Dr
Ryelaw
Champion Way
The Way
Curzon Dr
Fox Cft
Moore Rd
Moore Cl
Bowenhurst Road
Bowenhurst Gdns
Verne
Chesilton Crs
Ayesgarth
Foye La
Lion Way
Haig Lane
Azalea Gardens
Bakehouse Gdns
Redwoods Wy
Wynne Gdns
Tudor Wy
Cadet Way
Church Crookham Junior School
Tweseldown Infant School
Oaken Copse
Tweseldown Rd
Atbara Road
Oakwood
Hampton Cl
Works
Keynes Cl
Manor Ct
Sandy Lane
Earlsbourne
Kimberley
Hawkwell
BEACON HILL ROAD
Bourley Road
Chestnut Copse
Fleet Business Park
Wakefords Copse
Leipzig Road
Wakefords Pk
Leipzig Barracks
Lane
Tadpole
Ewshot Lane
Bourley Lane
Works
PO
P
E F G H
I 2 3 4 5
39 40 46 53
82 83
53 52 51

A
B
C
D
40
A323
Stirling
483
84
53
52
51
FLEET ROAD
Basingstoke Canal
Eelmoor Bridge
Laffan's Rd
Laffan
Track
Pavillion
Road
1
2
3
4
5
45
Long Valley
Ravine Head
Eelmoor Road
Plain Road
Eelmoor
Claycart Bottom
Claycart Road
Outridden Copse
Copse
P
Bourley Road
Bourley Lane
Bourley Road
Sunny Hill
Royal Pavili
54
1 grid square represents 500 metres

North Camp
Army Golf Club
Watts Common
Golf Course
Forge Lane
Laffan's Road
Shoe Lane
Vine Cl
Queen's Parade
Aldershot Garrison Sports Centre
Aldershot Military Stadium
Prince's
Basingstoke Canal
Browning Barracks
Airborne Forces Museum
Clubhouse Road
FLEET ROAD
A323
FARNBOROUGH ROAD
A325
Potters International Hotel
Rushmoor Arena
Rushmoor Bottom
GU11
Alison's Road
Pitts Road
Maida Rd
Hope Grant's Road
Steele's Road
Buller Rd
Mandora Rd
Montgomery Lines
Thornhill Crescent
Gallwey Rd
Arnhem Barracks
Pennefather's Road
Prince Consort's Library
Knollys Road
Bourley Road
Rushmoor Road
Hospital Road
Queen's Avenue
Scarlett's Rd
Duchess of Kent Barracks
Fire Station Rd
Aldershot Centre for Health
Middle Hill Health Clinic
Aldershot Outpatients
Campbell Rd
Rutland Cl
Talavera Junior School
Badajos Rd
Pakenham Dr
Cole Av
Willems Avenue
Superstore
WELLINGTON AVENUE
Police Station & Mag Court
Princes Hall
Surgery
High St
HIGH ST
The Kings Centre
Cassino Cl
Anzio Cl
Salerno Cl
Falaise Cl
Mareth Cl
Gun Hill
Ordnance Road
Telephone Exchange
Aldershot Town FC
Coltwood Bus Cen
Beaumont Junior School
Alexandra Road
Cambridge Road
Perowne St
Elizabeth Dr
Alxndr Rd
Union Street
Wellington Shopping Centre
Aldershot & Farnham Co-Ct
VICTORIA RD
QUEENS RD
Council Building
Community Centre
Birchett Rd
Auchinleck Wy
Alexandra
Infant School
Laburnum Rd
Elms Rd
Central Est
Aldershot Station
Beechnut Industrial Est
HIGH STREET
Western Rd
King's Rd
Kingsway
Sandford Road
YORK ROAD
Cargate Av
Works
GROSVENOR ROAD
B3007
Lysns Rd
Halimote Rd
Gordon Rd
Cavendish Rd
The Grove
Ascot Ct
St George's Rd
St Joseph's Rd
St Michael's Rd
Manor Park
Windmill Road
Waterloo Rd
Legge Crescent
Pavilion
Chetwode Ter
E
F
G
H
1
2
3
4
5
41
42
48
55
86
87
51
52
53

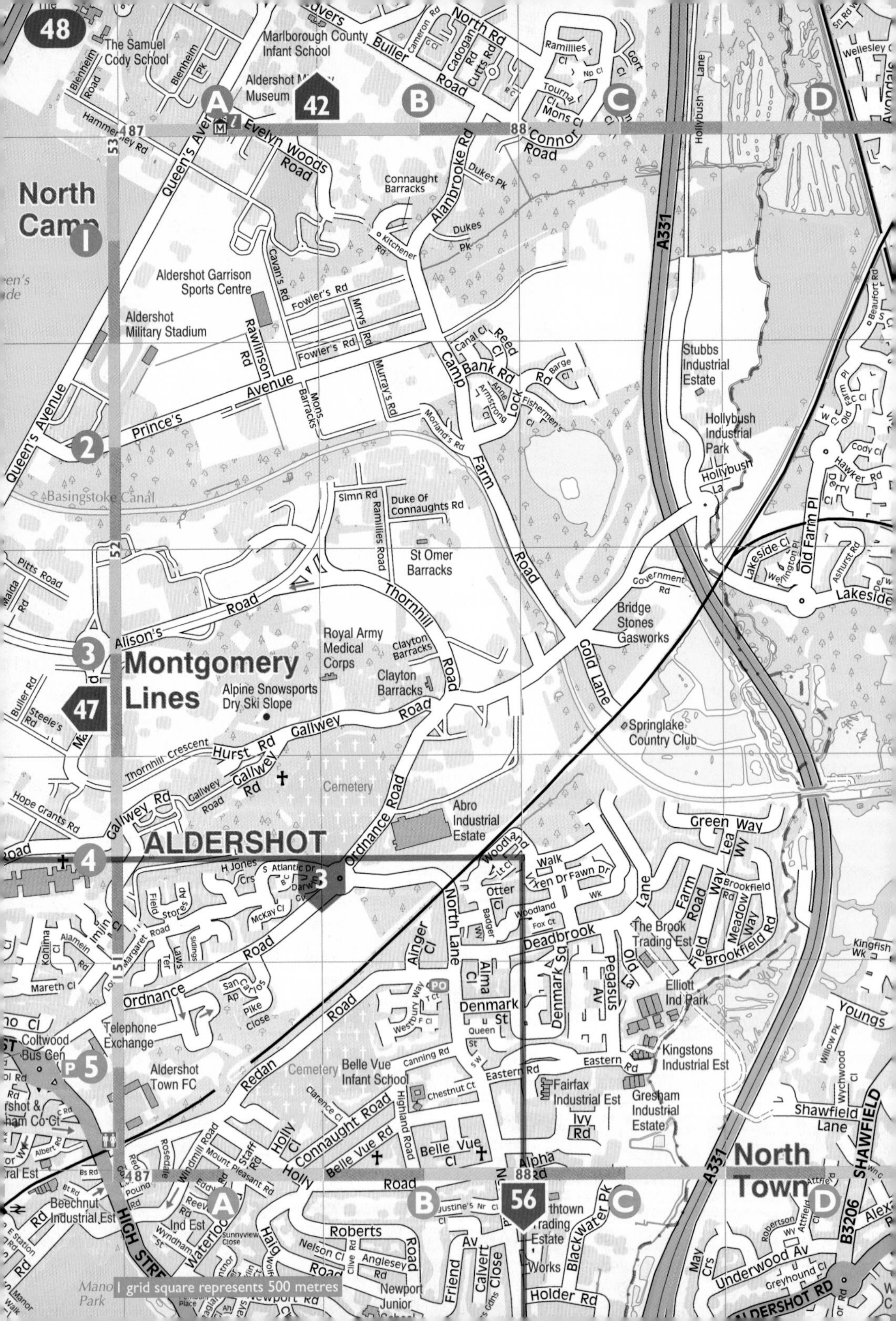
48
The Samuel Cody School
Marlborough County Infant School
Aldershot Military Museum
42
Buller Road
Cameron Rd
Cadogan Rd
Cutts Rd
North Rd
Ramillies Cl
Tournai Cl
Mons Cl
Gort Cl
Blenheim Road
Blenheim Pk
Hammersley Rd
Queen's Ave
Evelyn Woods Road
Connor Road
Alanbrooke Rd
Dukes Pk
Connaught Barracks
Kitchener Rd
North Camp
Aldershot Garrison Sports Centre
Aldershot Military Stadium
Cavan's Rd
Fowler's Rd
Rawlinson Rd
Murray's Rd
Prince's Avenue
Mons Barracks
Morland's Rd
Camp Farm Road
Canal Cl
Reed Cl
Bank Rd
Barge Cl
Lock Rd
Anne Armstrong Cl
Fishermen's Cl
Queen's Avenue
Basingstoke Canal
Slmn Rd
Duke Of Connaughts Rd
Ramillies Road
St Omer Barracks
Pitts Road
Maida Rd
Alison's Road
Thornhill Road
Government Rd
Bridge Stones Gasworks
Royal Army Medical Corps
Clayton Barracks
Montgomery Lines
Alpine Snowsports Dry Ski Slope
Gold Lane
Springlake Country Club
Buller Rd
Steele's Rd
47
Thornhill Crescent
Hurst Rd
Gallwey Road
Gallwey Rd
Cemetery
Ordnance Road
Abro Industrial Estate
Hope Grants Rd
ALDERSHOT
Green Way
Lea Wy
Woodland Walk
Vixen Dr
Fawn Dr
Otter Cl
H Jones Crs
Atlantic Dr
Stores Ap
McKay Cl
Imjin Cl
Kohima Cl
Alamein Rd
Margaret Road
Laws Ter
Sidings
Ainger Cl
North Lane
Badger Wy
Fox Ct
Deadbrook Lane
Farm Road
Field Way
Meadow Way
Brookfield Rd
The Brook Trading Est
Kingfisher Wk
Mareth Cl
San Carlos Ap
Pike Close
Alma Cl
Denmark Sq
Denmark St
Pegasus Av
Old La
Elliott Ind Park
Youngs
Telephone Exchange
Coltwood Bus Cen
Westbury Way
Queen St
Eastern Rd
Kingstons Industrial Est
Willow Pk
Wychwood
Aldershot Town FC
Redan Road
Cemetery
Canning Rd
Belle Vue Infant School
Chestnut Ct
Clarence Cl
Fairfax Industrial Est
Gresham Industrial Estate
Shawfield Lane
SHAWFIELD
Connaught Road
Highland Road
Holly Cl
Belle Vue Rd
Belle Vue Cl
Ivy Rd
North Town
A331
Windmill Road
Rosedale
Staff Rd
Mount Pleasant Rd
Holly Road
Alpha Rd
Beechnut Industrial Est
Reeves Rd
Ind Est
Waterloo
Justine's Cl
56
Northtown Trading Estate
Blackwater Pk
Robertson Wy
Attfield Cl
B3206
Wyndham
Sunnyview Close
Roberts Road
Nelson Cl
Anglesey Rd
Newport Junior School
Friend Av
Calvert Close
Works
Holder Rd
May Crs
Underwood Av
Greyhound Cl
ALDERSHOT RD
HIGH STREET
Manor Park
1 grid square represents 500 metres
Stubbs Industrial Estate
Hollybush Industrial Park
Hollybush La
Hollybush Lane
Lakeside Cl
Wellington Pl
Old Farm Pl
Ashurst Rd
Lakeside
Cody Cl
Hawker Rd
Derry Cl
Beaufort Rd
Wellesley
Avondale
487
88
53
52
51

Greatbottom Flash
Chart House Rd
Kestrel Cl
Wentworth Crs
Newfield Rd
Horseshoe
Ash Vale
Rowcroft Cl
Pine Cl
Heathvale Br Rd
Acre Road
Cuthbert Rd
Chambers Rd
Hutton Road
Jubilee Drive
Penrose Gdns
St Mary's Road
Springfield Rd
Prospect Road
Dorset Rd
Enfield Rd
Farm Rd
Scotland Cl
Orchard Cl
VALE ROAD
B3411
Elleray Ct
Gorselands Cl
Crescent Lane
Foxhurst Rd
Oaklea
Chandlers Rd
Ash Vale Health Cen
Newlands Dr
Npr La
Burrwood Gdns
Mulberry
Wharf Road
Grenadier Rd
Woollards Road
Balmoral Road
VALE RD
GU12
Ash Common
Wyke Comm
PO
Shawfield Primary School
Beeton's Av
Church Pth
Grove Rd
College Road
Cross Rd
Hillside Road
ASH HILL ROAD
Winchester Rd
Chichester Rd
York Rd
Canterbury Rd
Grange Farm Rd
Old School Cl
Heathcote Rd
Fairview Road
Ash Cl
Beeching Cl
Elm Vw
Miles Rd
Wren Ct
ASH HILL RD
Brackendene
Upr Pinewood Road
Nightingale Rd
Pinewood Rd
Kirriemuir Gdns
Fox Hills Lane
Ashbourne Close
Ravenscroft Close
GUILDFORD ROAD
A323
Dene Cl
Wyke Avenue
Wyke Lane
Ash
Exeter Rd
Murrell Rd
Ashdene Crs
Ashdene Rd
Salisbury Rd
York Road
Potters Crs
Chester Rd
Chester Cl
Ash Grange CP School
Cem
Ewins Cl
Longacre
Church View
Britten Cl
Ash Station
ASH CHURCH RD
LC
East Wyke Farm
Harper's Road
Longfield Road
Manfield Rd
Collins Gdns
Church La
St Peters Md
Foreman Pk
Foreman Road
Old Rectory Dr
Grange Road
ASH STREET
Old Chapel La
Southlands Cl
Loddon Way
Lea Cl
Southlands Rd
Ash Ldg Cl
Littlefield Cl
Wey Cl
Colne Wy
Wandle Cl
Parish Cl
Brambles Cl
Whitethorn Cl
Willow Flds
Ash Green Road
Pound Farm
E F G H
1 2 3 4 5
90 91
43 50 57
53 52 151

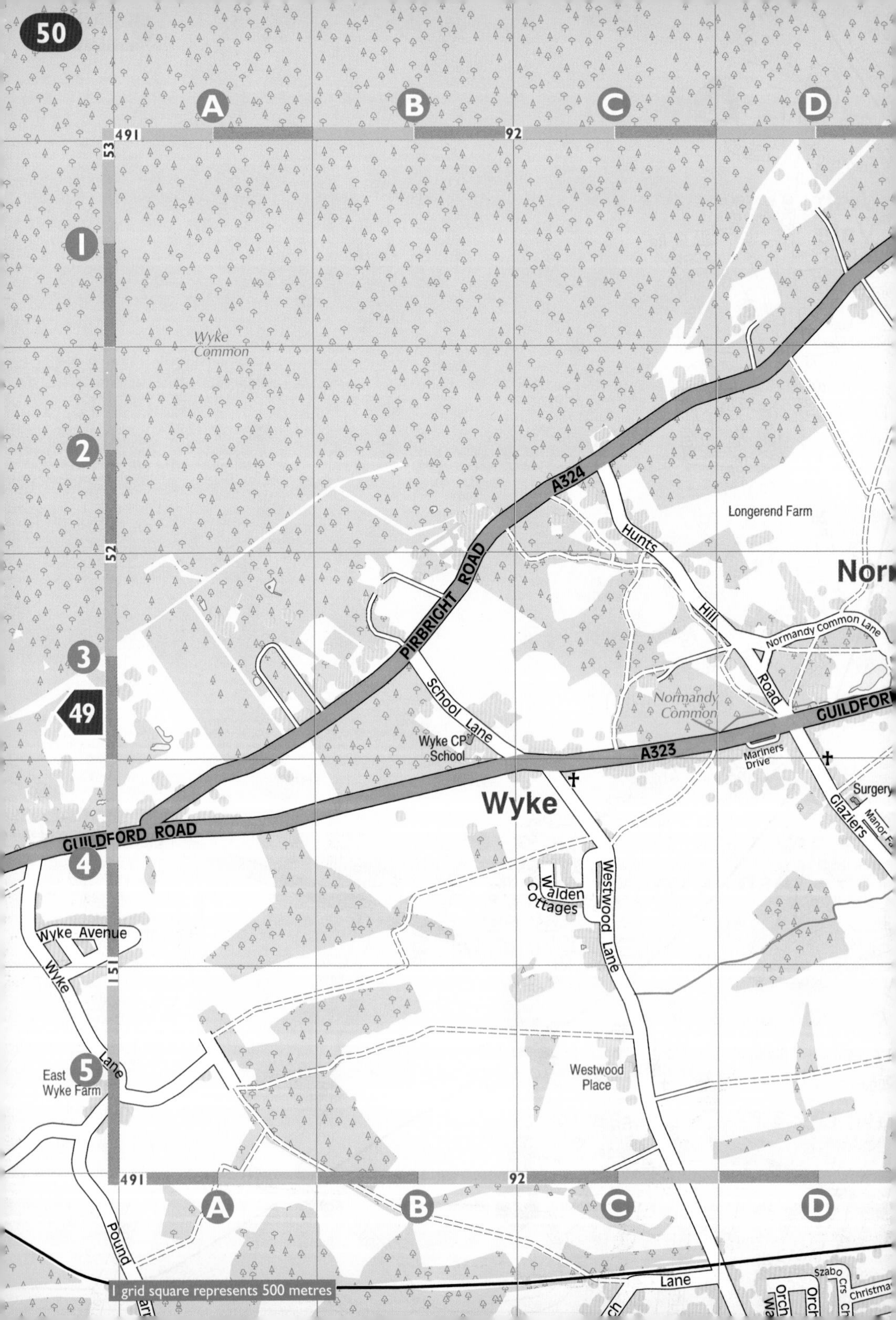
A
B
C
D
491
92
53
52
51
1
2
3
4
5
49
Wyke Common
A324
PIRBRIGHT ROAD
Longerend Farm
Hunts Hill Road
Norr
Normandy Common Lane
Normandy Common
GUILDFORD
A323
School Lane
Wyke CP School
Mariners Drive
Surgery
Glaziers
Manor Fa
Wyke
GUILDFORD ROAD
Walden Cottages
Westwood Lane
Wyke Avenue
Wyke Lane
East Wyke Farm
Westwood Place
Pound
Lane
Szabo Crs
Christma
Orch
1 grid square represents 500 metres

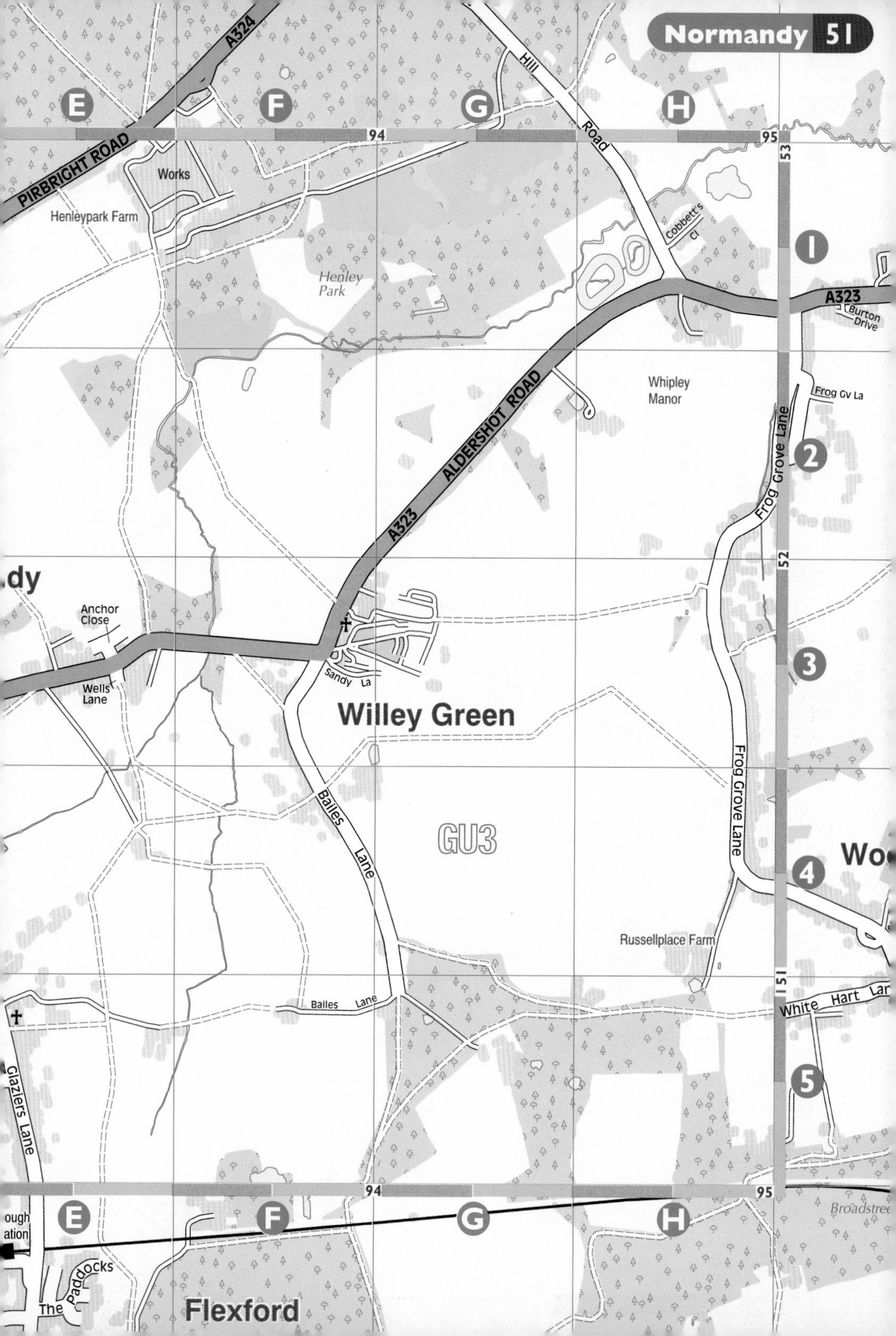
A324
PIRBRIGHT ROAD
Works
Henleypark Farm
Hill Road
Cobbett's Cl
Henley Park
A323
Burton Drive
ALDERSHOT ROAD
Whipley Manor
Frog Gv La
Frog Grove Lane
Anchor Close
Wells Lane
Sandy La
Willey Green
Bailes Lane
GU3
Russellplace Farm
White Hart Lane
Glaziers Lane
The Paddocks
Flexford
Broadstree
E
F
G
H
94
95
53
52
51
1
2
3
4
5

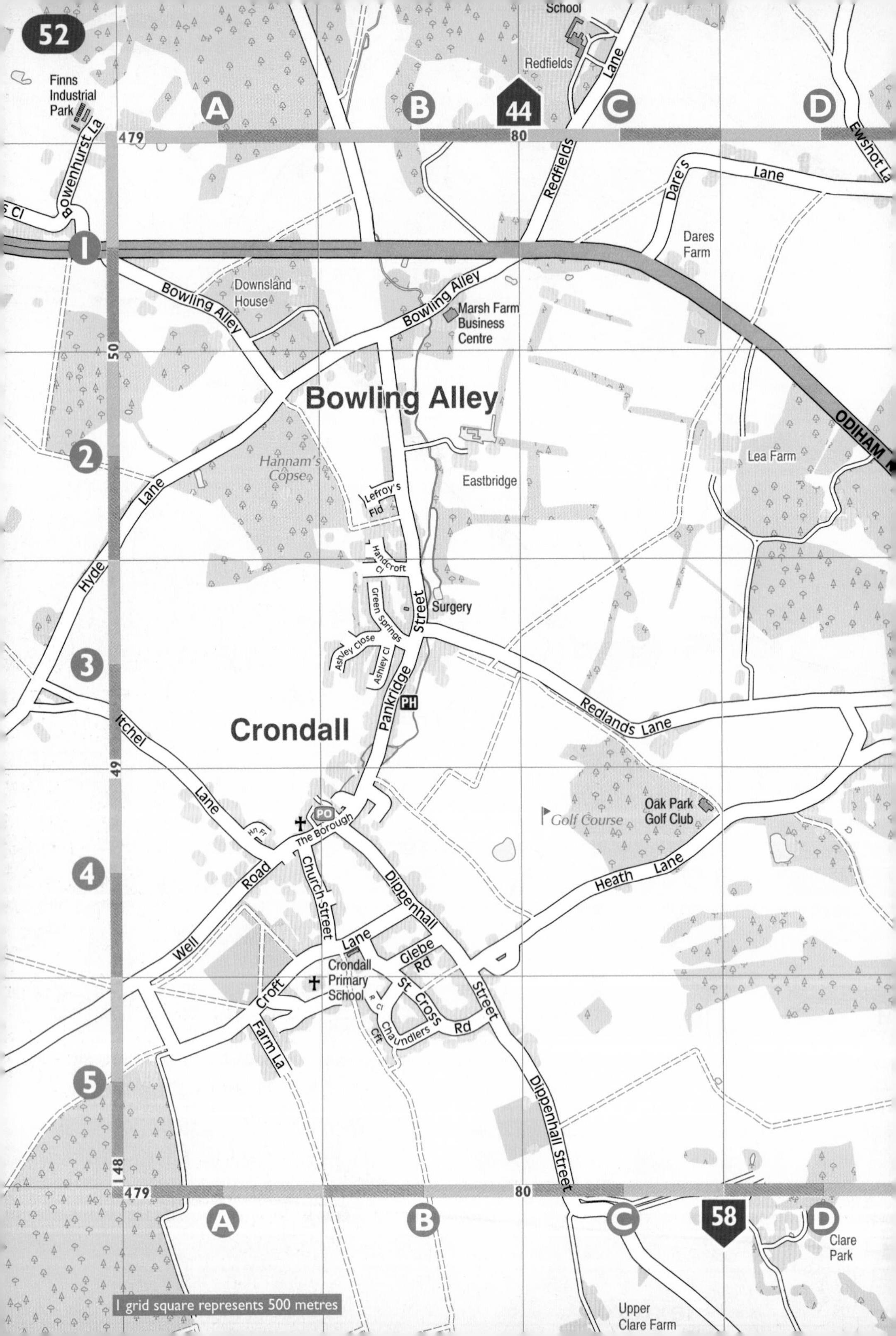

Finns Industrial Park
Bowenhurst La
School
Redfields
Lane
44
A
B
C
D
479
80
Redfields
Dare's
Lane
Ewshot La
Dares Farm
Bowling Alley
Downsland House
Bowling Alley
Marsh Farm Business Centre
50
Bowling Alley
ODIHAM
Hannam's Copse
Lea Farm
Lane
Lefroy's Fld
Eastbridge
Handcroft Cl
Hyde
Green Springs
Street
Surgery
Ashley Close
Ashley Cl
Pankridge
PH
Redlands Lane
Itchel
Crondall
49
Lane
Oak Park Golf Club
Golf Course
PO
The Borough
Hn Ft
Road
Church Street
Dippenhall
Heath Lane
Well
Lane
Glebe Rd
Crondall Primary School
Croft
St Cross Rd
Street
Farm La
R Cl
Chaundlers Cft
Dippenhall Street
148
479
80
58
Clare Park
1 grid square represents 500 metres
Upper Clare Farm

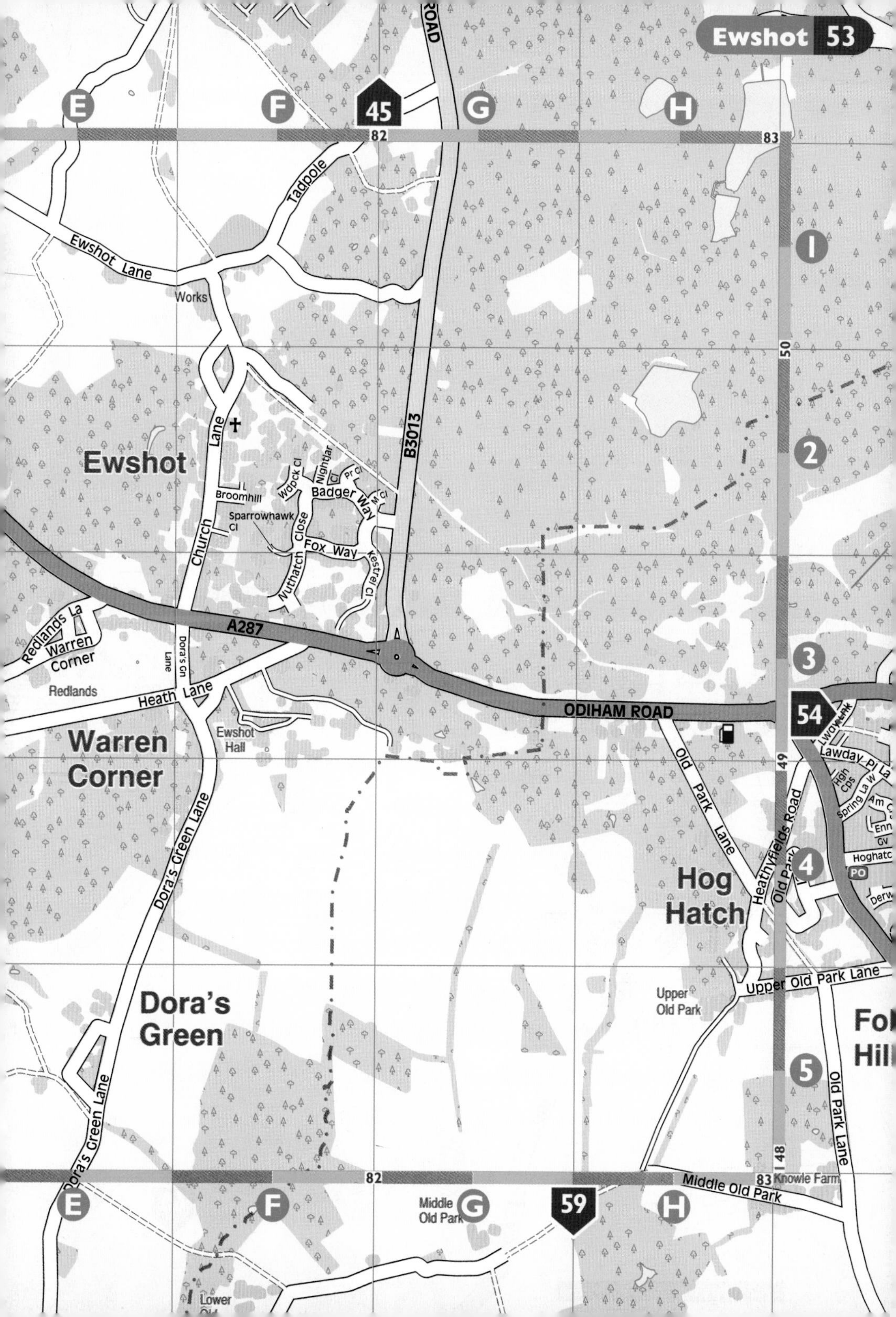

E
F
45
G
H
82
83
I
2
3
4
5
50
49
48
ROAD
Tadpole
Ewshot Lane
Works
Ewshot
Church Lane
Broomhill
Sparrowhawk Cl
Wapck Cl
Nightjar Cl
Pr Cl
Badger Way
M Cl
Close
Fox Way
Nuthatch
Kestrel Cl
B3013
A287
Redlands La
Warren Corner
Dora's Gn Lane
Redlands
Heath Lane
Ewshot Hall
ODIHAM ROAD
54
Warren Corner
Old Park Lane
Lawday Pl La
Heathyfields Road
Old Park
Hog Hatch
Hoghatc
PO
Upper Old Park Lane
Upper Old Park
Dora's Green Lane
Dora's Green
Fo
Hil
Old Park Lane
Knowle Farm
Middle Old Park
Middle Old Park
59
Lower

54
Bourley Lane
Works
A
B
46
C
D
483
84
50
49
48
1
2
3
4
5
53
59
60
Hampshire County
Surrey County
FARNBOROUGH ROAD
Bricksbury Hl
ALMA LANE
Sandy Hill Road
Eton Pl
Lyall Pl
Macdonald Rd
Sandford Rd
Swift Rd
Perry Wy
Brougham Pl
Blackheath Rd
Barrie Rd
Hale Primary School
Upper Hale Cemetery
B3005
UPPER HALE ROAD
Queens La
Wellesley Gdn
Ball and Wicket La
Yolland Cl
Vicarage Lane
Heath Lane
Wood Rd
The Green
Nutshell La
Parkside
The Gln
Highlands Rd
The Dell
Elm Crs
Elm Gv
Elm Rd
Hill Rd
Alma Way
Poplar Wk
The Glade
Queen Anne's Gate
Rushden Wy
Bethel La
Bethel Cl
North Av
West Cl
West Av
East Av
South Av
Willow Way
White Cottage Cl
Fairview Gdns
The Charlotte Crescent
Santina Cl
Nelson Cl
Nelson Rd
Works
Wellington La
The Fairway
A3016
Oast House Lane
Hale
Spring La
Lawday Pl La
Newmans Ct
Parish Cl
Gravel Rd
Bishops Rd
Folly Lane North
Hope La
Hereford La
Fernhill La
Fernhill Dr
Wings Cl
Wings Rd
Grasmere Rd
Windermere Way
Hillbrook Rl
Trinity Hill
Farnham Pk Cl
Shady Nook
Hoghatch La
Coniston Dr
Derwent Cl
Infant School
Drovers Wy
Hampton Road
Windsor Crs
Blenheim Crs
Upper Hale
Hog Hatch
Heathyfields Road
Old Park Cl
Old Park Lane
Upper Old Park Lane
Upper Old Park
Folly Hill
FOLLY HILL
A287
Old Park Lane
Middle Old Park
Farnham Park
Golf Course
1 grid square represents 500 metres

Weybourne
Badshot Lea
WELLINGTON AVENUE
VICTORIA RD
HIGH ST
Aldershot Station
Wellington Shopping Centre
Council Building
Beaumont Junior School
Infant School
Alexandra Road
Cambridge Road
Sandford Road
YORK ROAD
CRANMORE LANE
B3008
GROSVENOR ROAD
B3007
Birchett Rd
Elms Rd
Lysons Rd
Cargate Av
Church Lane West
Manor Rd
Bourne Ct
Ayling Lane
Rowhill Avenue
Hillside Road
EGGAR'S HILL
BOXALL'S LANE
Bridge Rd
St Josephs Catholic Prim Sch
Highfield Avenue
Highfield Gdns
St George's Rd
St Michael's Rd
Manor Park
Beechnut Industrial Est
Northbrook Rd
Brockenhurst Rd
Avondale Rd
Church Lane
Evelyn Avenue
St Michaels CE Junior School
St Michaels CE Infant Sch
Park Road
Jubilee Road
Coronation Road
Church Road
Windmill Road
Waterloo Rd
A323
A325
Copse Avenue
Oakland Avenue
Woodbourne
Woodside Road
Weybourne Road
B3007
All Hallows Catholic School
Lower Weybourne Lane
Farnham Heath End School
William Cobbett Junior School
Preymead Industrial Estate
LOWER FARNHAM ROAD
B3208
Park Primary School
Surgery
Badshot Lea Village Infant School
Badshot Park
BADSHOT LEA ROAD
Garden Centre
St Georges Road
Low Lane
Crown Lane
Pine View Cl
Green Lane
WEYBOURNE ROAD
MONKTON LANE
B3367
Works
Cemetery
WATER LA
Bus Cen
Farnham Trading Estate
Superstore
Badshot Farm
Runfold St George
The Willows
47
56
61
E
F
G
H
I
1
2
3
4
5
86
87
50
49
48

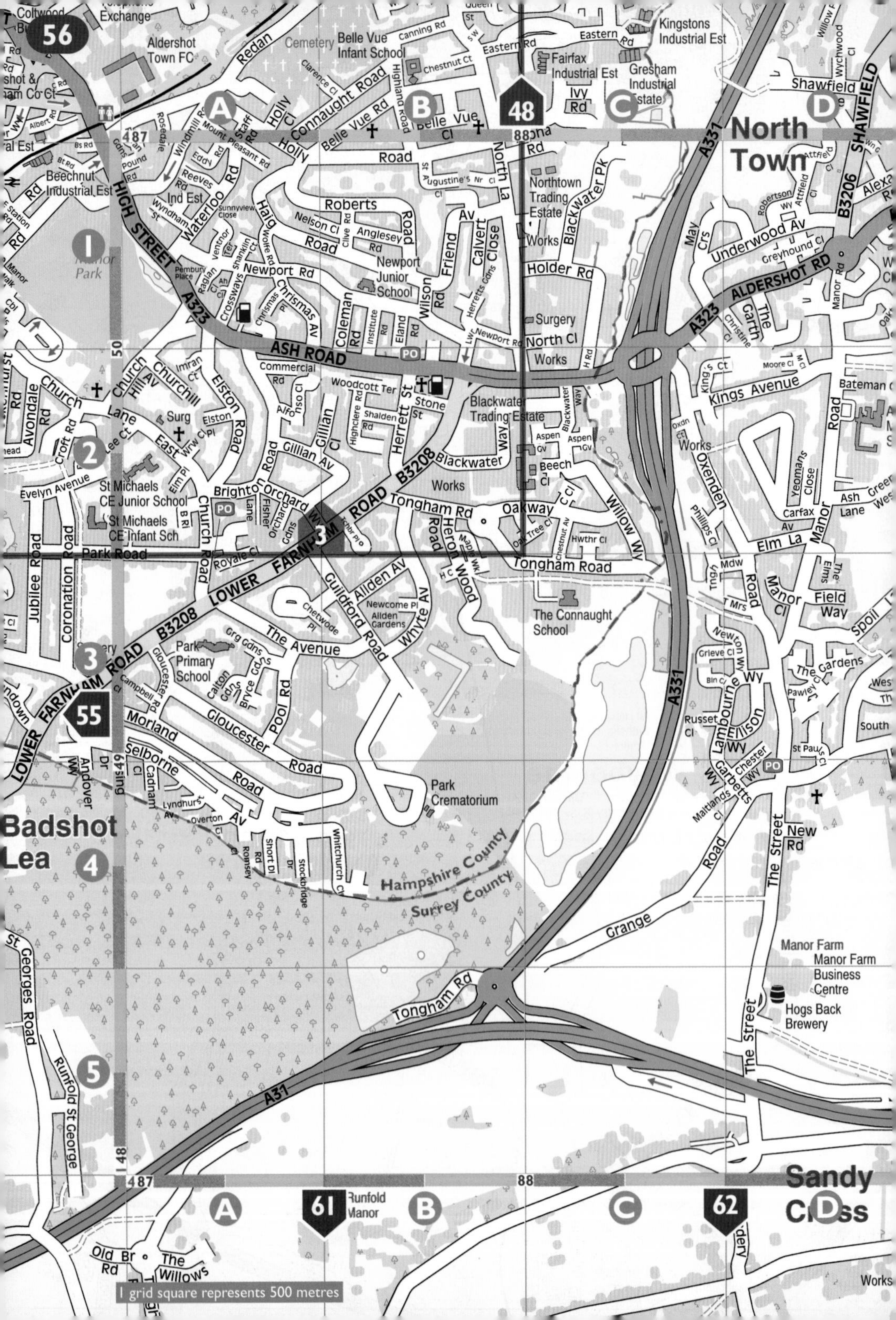

56
Aldershot Town FC
Cemetery
Redan
Belle Vue Infant School
Canning Rd
Eastern Rd
Kingstons Industrial Est
Fairfax Industrial Est
Gresham Industrial Estate
Clarence Cl
Connaught Road
Highland Road
Chestnut Ct
Ivy Rd
A
B
C
D
48
Shawfield
Shawfield
North Town
487
88
Holly
Belle Vue Rd
Belle Vue
Cl
Road
North La
Rd
Mount Pleasant Rd
Windmill Rd
Rosedale
Staff
Pound
Beechnut Industrial Est
HIGH STREET
Reeves Rd
Ind Est
Waterloo Rd
Wyndham St
Eddy Rd
St Augustine's Cl
Northtown Trading Estate
Blackwater Pk
A331
Roberts Road
Nelson Cl
Clive Rd
Anglesey Rd
Road
Friend Av
Calvert Close
Works
Holder Rd
May Crs
Robertson Wy
Attfield Cl
B3206
Alexa
Underwood Av
Greyhound Cl
ALDERSHOT RD
1
Manor Park
Haig Rd
Wolfe Rd
Sunnyview Close
Ventnor Ter
Shanklin Ct
Newport Rd
Newport Junior School
Wilson Rd
Herretts Gdns
Surgery
Pembury Place
Raglan Cl
Crossways
Chrismas Pl
Chrismas Av
Coleman Rd
Institute Rd
Eland Rd
Newport Rd
North Cl
A323
Christine Cl
The Garth
Manor Rd
50
ASH ROAD
PO
Commercial Rd
Works
H Rd
Moore Cl
King's Ct
Kings Avenue
Bateman
Church Hill Av
Churchill Av
Imran Ct
Elston Road
Woodcott Ter
Stone St
Blackwater Trading Estate
Blackwater Way
Avondale Rd
Church Lane East
Surg
Elston Pl
Alfonso Cl
Gillian Cl
Highclere Rd
Shalden Rd
Herrett St
Aspen Gv
Oxenden Ct
Works
Road
Croft Rd
Lee Ct
Gillian Av
Blackwater Way
Beech Cl
Oxenden Road
Yeomans Close
2
Evelyn Avenue
St Michaels CE Junior School
St Michaels CE Infant Sch
Elm Pl
B3208
Works
Brighton Rd
Orchard Wy
Fisher Lane
Orchard Gdns
Church Road
Tongham Rd
Oakway
Willow Wy
Oak Tree Cl
Chestnut Av
Phillips Cl
Carfax Av
Ash Green Lane West
Manor
Elm La
Jubilee Road
Coronation Road
Park Road
Royale Cl
3
Heron Wood Road
Maple Wk
Tongham Road
Hawthorn Cl
LOWER FARNHAM ROAD
Alden Av
Chetwode Pl
Guildford Road
Newcome Pl
Alden Gardens
Whyte Av
The Connaught School
Meadow
T Mrs
Manor Cl
Field Way
The Elms
Spoil
Park Primary School
The Avenue
Gloucester Rd
Campbell Rd
Calton Gdns
Bryce Gdns
Pool Rd
3
55
Gloucester Road
Morland
Newton Wy
Grieve Cl
Lambourne Wy
Ellison Wy
Russet Cl
The Gardens
Pawley Cl
South
St Pauls Cl
Selborne Road
Cadnam Cl
Andover Wy
Lyndhurst Av
Overton Cl
Av
Romsey Rd
Short Dl
Stockbridge Dr
Whitchurch Cl
Park Crematorium
Chester Wy
Garbetts Wy
Maitlands Cl
New Rd
The Street
Badshot Lea
4
49
Hampshire County
Surrey County
Grange Road
Manor Farm
Manor Farm Business Centre
Hogs Back Brewery
St Georges Road
Runfold St George
5
Tongham Rd
A31
The Street
48
487
88
61
Runfold Manor
62
Sandy Cross
Old Br Rd
The Willows
Works
1 grid square represents 500 metres

Ash Station
Wyke Farm
Longacre
Church View
ASH CHURCH RD
A323
Collins Gdns
St Peters
Foreman Pk
49
Rectory Dr
Harper's
ASH STREET
Grange Road
Southlands Cl
Southlands Rd
South Lane
Loddon Way
Littlefield Gdns
Lea Cl
Ash Ldg Cl
Wey Cl
Colne Wy
Wandle Cl
Parish Cl
Brambles Cl
Willow Flds
Foreman Road
Whitethorn Cl
Kennet Cl
Lodge Dr
The Briars
Ash Green Road
Drovers Way
White Lane
Pound Farm Lane
Farm Green
Ash Green La East
Old Farm Wk
Cross Tree Wy
Pilgrims Vw
Ash Green
Hazel Road
Poyle Farm
St Pauls CE Infant School
Poyle Road
Poyle Rd
White Lane
gham
White Lane Farm
Inwood Fa
Ramada Hotel
HOG'S BACK A31
Hog's Back
Elstead Road
Wood Lane
Seale
Seale Lane
Puttenham Road
School Hill
63
E F G H
1 2 3 4 5
90 91
50 49 48

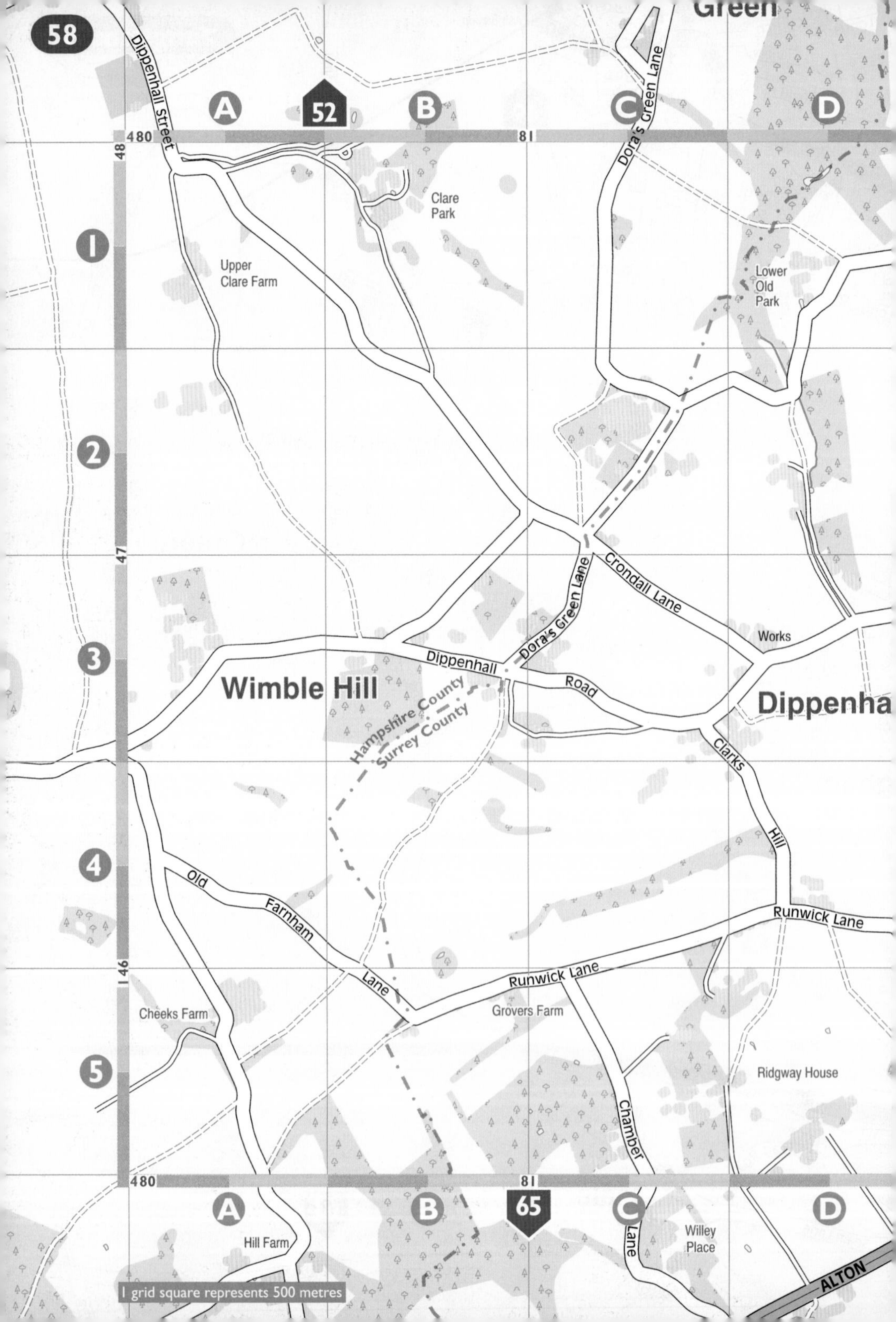
Green
52
A
B
C
D
480
81
48
47
46
1
2
3
4
5
Dippenhall Street
Dora's Green Lane
Clare Park
Upper Clare Farm
Lower Old Park
Crondall Lane
Works
Dippenhall
Road
Wimble Hill
Dippenha
Hampshire County
Surrey County
Clarks
Hill
Old
Farnham
Lane
Runwick Lane
Cheeks Farm
Grovers Farm
Ridgway House
Chamber
Lane
65
Hill Farm
Willey Place
ALTON
1 grid square represents 500 metres

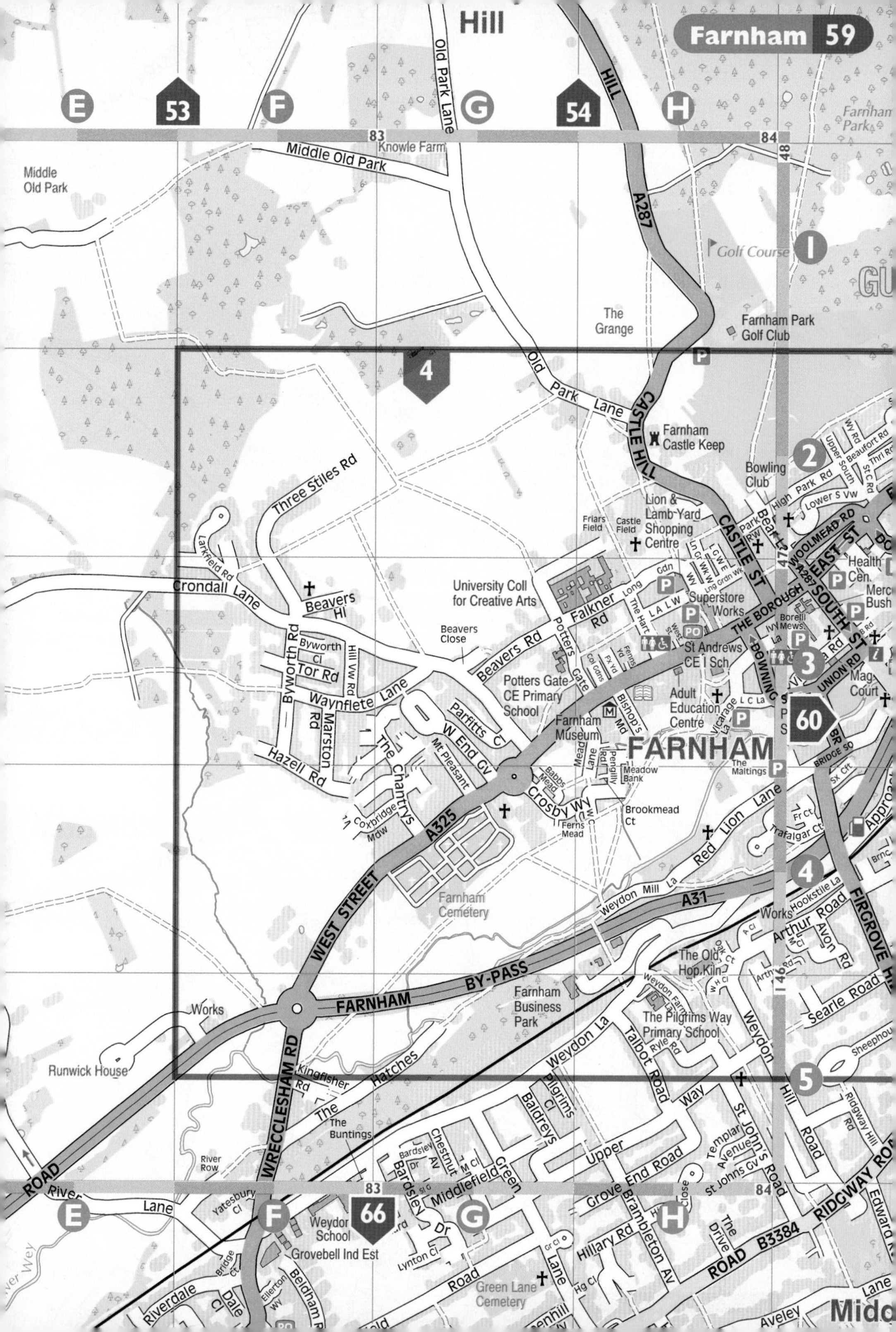
Hill
Middle Old Park
Knowle Farm
Old Park Lane
Castle Hill
A287
Golf Course
The Grange
Farnham Park Golf Club
Farnham Park
Farnham Castle Keep
Bowling Club
Three Stiles Rd
Crondall Lane
Larkfield Rd
Beavers Hl
Byworth Rd
Byworth Cl
Tor Rd
Hill Vw Rd
Waynflete Lane
Marston Rd
Hazell Rd
The Chantrys
Coxbridge Mdw
W End Gv
Mt Pleasant
Parfitts Cl
Beavers Close
Beavers Rd
University Coll for Creative Arts
Falkner Rd
Potters Gate
Potters Gate CE Primary School
Farnham Museum
Bishop's Md
Friars Field
Castle Field
Lion & Lamb Yard Shopping Centre
Castle St
The Borough
Downing St
Woolmead Rd
East St
South St
Union Rd
Health Cen.
Mag Court
Superstore
Works
St Andrews CE I Sch
Adult Education Centre
Vicarage La
FARNHAM
The Maltings
Meadow Bank
Brookmead Ct
Crosby Wy
Ferns Mead
Babbs Mead
Mead Lane
Red Lion Lane
Trafalgar Ct
Weydon Mill La
A31
A325
West Street
Farnham Cemetery
Farnham By-Pass
Farnham Business Park
The Old Hop Kiln
Arthur Road
Avon Rd
Firgrove Hill
Searle Road
Hookstile La
Weydon La
Talbot Road
The Pilgrims Way Primary School
Weydon Hill Road
Works
Runwick House
Wrecclesham Rd
Kingfisher Rd
The Hatches
The Buntings
River Row
River Lane
Yatesbury Cl
Weydon School
Grovebell Ind Est
Riverdale
Dale Cl
Beldham Rd
Bardsley Dr
Chestnut Av
Middlefield
Green Road
Lynton Cl
Green Lane Cemetery
Baldreys
Pilgrims Cl
Upper Way
Grove End Road
Brambleton Av
Hillary Rd
The Drive
St John's Road
St Johns Gv
Templar Avenue
Ridgway Road
Ridgway Hill Rd
B3384
Edward Rd
Aveley
Sheephouse
Road
Approach
Bridge Sq
Mid
GU
53
54
4
60
66
83
84
47
46
48
E
F
G
H
I
2
3
4
5

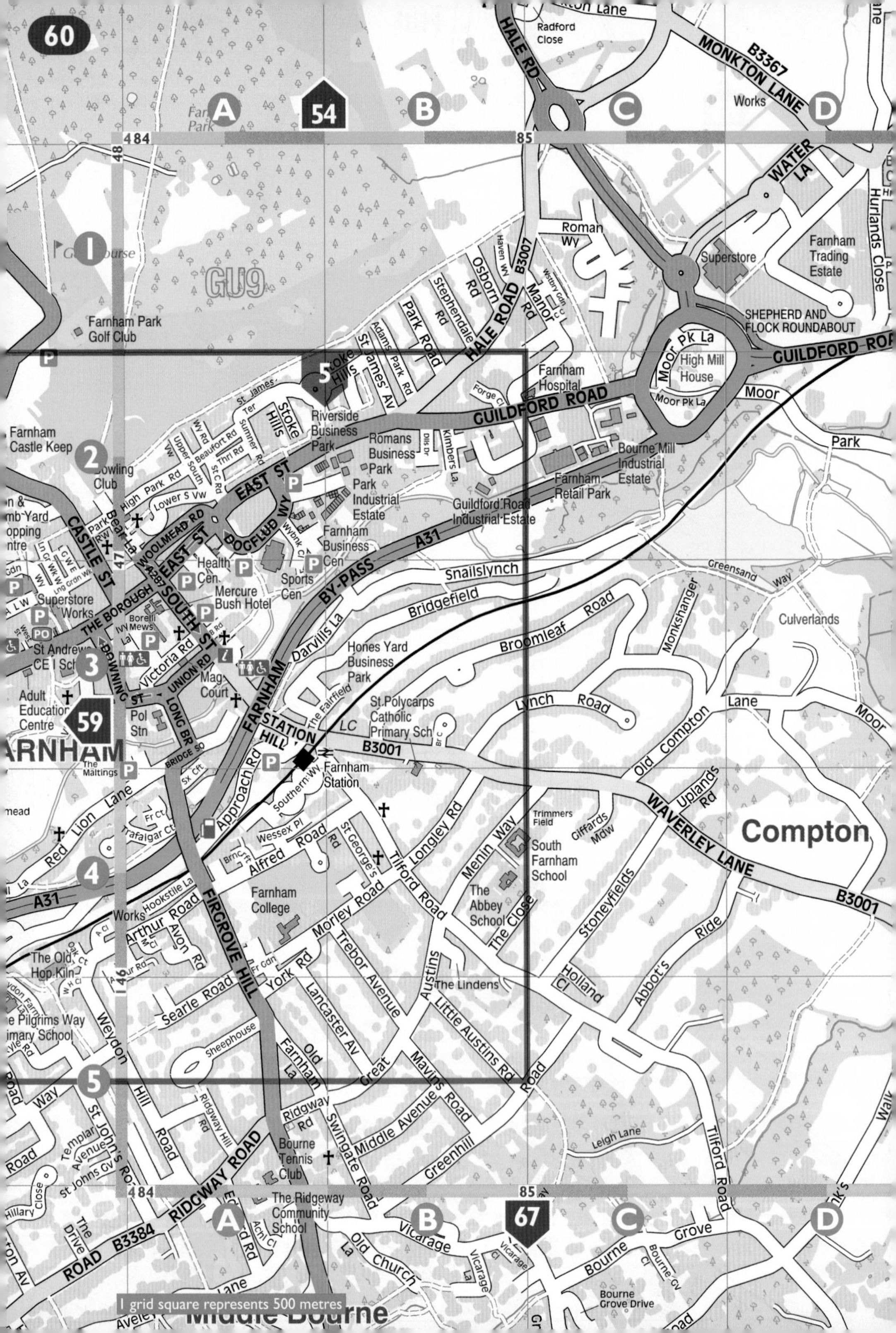
60
54
59
67
5
A
B
C
D
1
2
3
4
5
484
85
48
47
46
Radford Close
HALE RD
MONKTON LANE
B3367
Works
WATER LA
Hurlands Close
Farnham Trading Estate
Superstore
Roman Wy
Haven Wy
B3007
Osborn Rd
Stephendale Rd
Manor Rd
Wstbry Gdn
HALE ROAD
Park Road
Adams Park Rd
St James' Av
Stoke Hills
GU9
Farnham Park Golf Club
SHEPHERD AND FLOCK ROUNDABOUT
GUILDFORD ROAD
Moor Pk La
High Mill House
Moor Park
Farnham Hospital
Forge Cl
Riverside Business Park
Romans Business Park
Park Industrial Estate
Kimbers La
Bourne Mill Industrial Estate
Farnham Retail Park
Guildford Road Industrial Estate
Farnham Castle Keep
Bowling Club
High Park Rd
Beaufort Rd
Upper South Vw
Thrl Rd
St C Rd
Summer Ter
Lower S Vw
EAST ST
DOGFLUD WY
WOOLMEAD RD
CASTLE ST
Bear La
Farnham Business Cen
A31
BY-PASS
Health Cen
Sports Cen
Mercure Bush Hotel
Snailslynch
Bridgefield
Greensand Way
Culverlands
Monkshanger
Darvills La
Broomleaf Road
Hones Yard Business Park
THE BOROUGH
SOUTH ST
Superstore Works
Borelli Mews
Ivy La
St Andrews CE I Sch
DOWNING ST
Victoria Rd
UNION RD
Mag Court
Adult Education Centre
Pol Stn
LONG BR
BRIDGE SQ
FARNHAM
STATION HILL
The Fairfield
St.Polycarps Catholic Primary Sch
LC
Lynch Road
Old Compton Lane
Moor
B3001
Farnham Station
Southern Wy
The Maltings
Approach Rd
Red Lion Lane
Fr Ct
Trafalgar Ct
Wessex Pl
Alfred Road
St George's Rd
Longley Rd
Tilford Road
Menin Way
Trimmers Field
Giffards Mdw
Uplands Rd
WAVERLEY LANE
Compton
South Farnham School
The Abbey School
The Close
Stoneyfields
Hookstile La
Works
Arthur Road
Avon Rd
Farnham College
Morley Road
FIRGROVE HILL
Trebor Avenue
Abbot's Ride
Holland Cl
The Old Hop Kiln
Oak Ct
York Rd
Fr Gdn
Searle Road
Lancaster Av
Austins
Little Austins Rd
The Lindens
Pilgrims Way Primary School
Weydon Hill Road
Sheephouse
Old Farnham La
Great Austins
Mavins Road
Road
Tilford Road
Leigh Lane
Ridgway Rd
Ridgway Hill Rd
Swingate Road
Middle Avenue
Greenhill
St John's Rd
Templar Avenue
St Johns Gv
RIDGWAY ROAD
Bourne Tennis Club
The Ridgeway Community School
Hillary Close
The Drive
ROAD B3384
Achl Cl
Vicarage La
Old Church La
Bourne Grove
Bourne Gv
Bourne Grove Drive
Middle Bourne
1 grid square represents 500 metres

ADSHOT
Runfold St George
A31
E
55
F
G
56
H
87
88
48
Badshot Farm
Runfold Manor
Old Br Rd
The Willows
Tongham Rd
I
Seale Lane
Guildford Road
Works
Guildford Road
Crooksbury Road
Barfield School
Runfold
Brookley Close
2
Lane
47
Sands Road
Blighton
Farnham Golf Club
Golf Course
3
The Sands
62
North Downs Way
Greenacres
Crooksbury Road
Compton Way
Sands Cl
Compton Way
The Green
Campana Finishing School
Moor Park
Swift's Cl
Botany Hill
4
River Wey (North Branch)
Temple's Close
Way
Smugglers'
46
Cobbets Rdg
Hill
Greensand Way
Monks' Well
Crooksbury Road
5
B3001
Camp
Waverley Abbey House
WAVERLEY LANE
87
88
E
F
G
H

62
56
61
A
B
C
D
1
2
3
4
5
488
89
48
47
46
Sandy Cross
Seale
The Sands
Ramada Hotel
HOG'S BACK
Elstead Road
Wood Lane
Seale Lane
Thundery Hill
Puttenham
School Hill
Works
North Downs Way
Lane
Blighton
Farnham Golf Club
Golf Course
Binton Lane
Binton Farm
Owlshatch
Sands Cl
The Green
Hill
Smugglers' Way
Littleworth Road
Long Hill
Seale Road
Littleworth Cross
Road
Crooksbury Common
1 grid square represents 500 metres

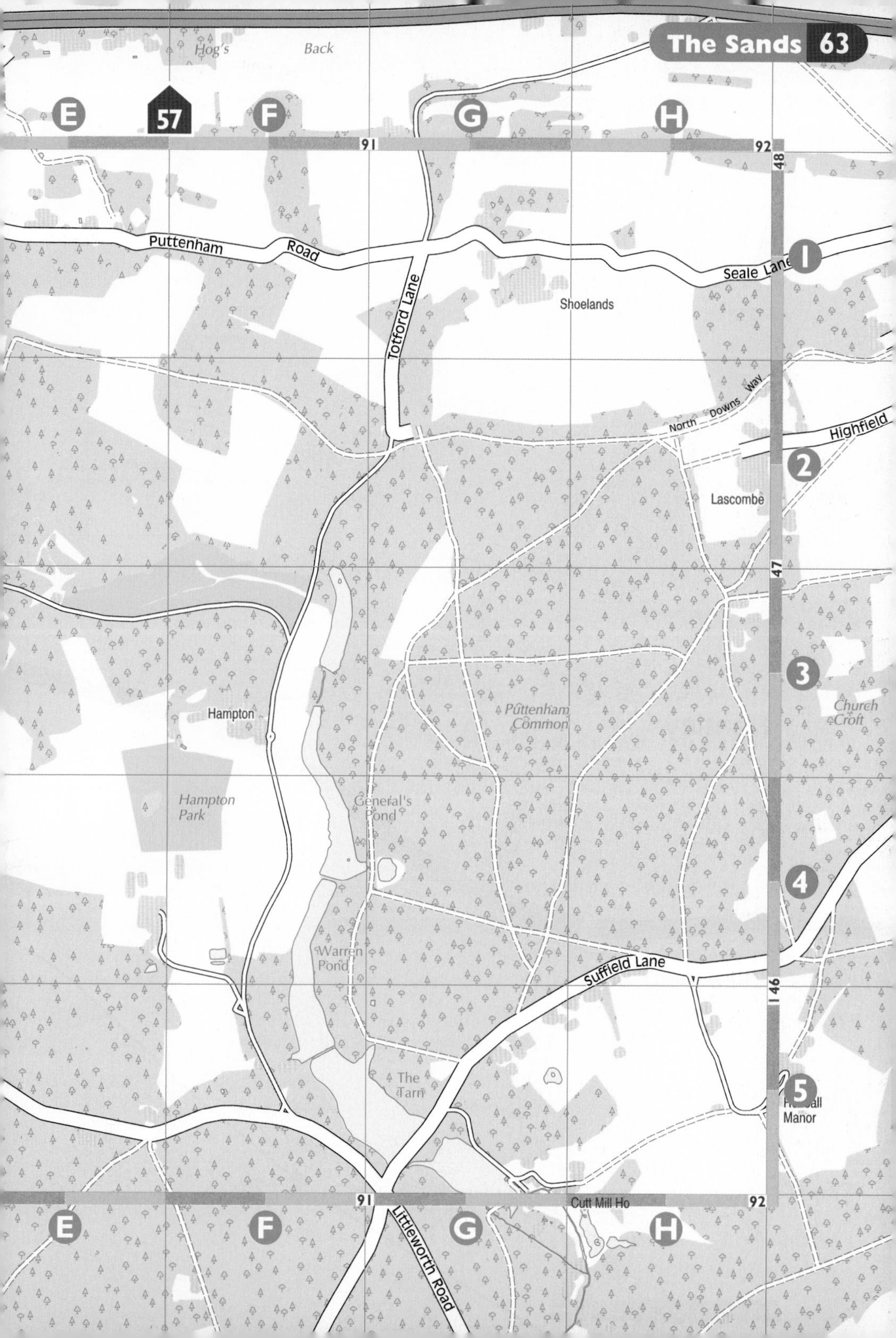
Hog's
Back
E
57
F
G
H
91
92
48
Puttenham
Road
I
Seale Lane
Totford Lane
Shoelands
North
Downs
Way
Highfield
2
Lascombe
47
3
Church
Croft
Hampton
Puttenham
Common
Hampton
Park
General's
Pond
4
Warren
Pond
Suffield Lane
46
The
Tarn
5
Manor
91
Cutt Mill Ho
92
E
F
G
H
Littleworth Road

A
B
C
D
478
79
45
44
43
1
2
3
4
5
Bury Court
Perryland
East Green
Marsh House
Church Lane
Hole Lane
School Lane
Jenkyn Place
Bentley CE Primary School
x Hill
Longcroft
Hole Lane
Babs Flds
Eggars Fld
Brdlnds Cl
Bentley
A31
Bonners Fld
Bus Park
Oakway
PO
Rectory Lane
Bentley Industrial Cen
Pax Hl
Works
The Drift
Station Road
Bentley Green Farm
Wey Bank
Bentley Station
Station Road
Isington Road
Isington
1 grid square represents 500 metres

Ridgway House
wick
E
F
58
G
H
81
82
Hill Farm
Lane
Willey Place
ROAD
River
Wey
ALTON
Crondall Road
Northbrook
45
2
A31
PH
WRECCLESHAM HILL
Works
B338
el Hill Road
Wrecclesham Hill
Holt Pound Lane
3
66
44
A325
4
Holt Pound Inclosure
Holt Pound
Works
Rosemary La
Fullers Road
Forest Glade
School Rd
High
Gravel Hill Road
Rowledge C (Controlled Prim School
5
Recreation Rd
PO
Cherry Tree Rd
Prosp Rd
Birdworld & Underwaterworld
Church La
Garden Centre
43
Works
81
82
E
F
G
H
Lodge Pond
Lickfolds
Alice Holt Lodge
Park Cl

Runwick House
The Hatches
Kingfisher Rd
The Bunt
River Row
Yatesbury Cl
Weydon School
Grovebell Ind Est
The Old Orchard
Lynton Cl
Middlefield
Green Lane
Baldreys
Pilgrims Cl
Upper
Grove End Rd
Brambleton Av
Hillary Rd
Hillary Close
Green Lane Cemetery
ALTON ROAD
River Lane
River Wey
Riverdale
Dale Cl
Bridge Ct
Ellerton Wy
Beldham Rd
School Hill
Buttermer Cl
Keable Rd
Stewards Rise
Works
Beales La
Greenfield Road
Little Green Lane
St Peters CE (Aided) Prim School
Cobbetts Way
Little Gn La
Greenhill Wy
Firfield Road
SHORTHEATH
B3384
Brockhurst Ldg
Cedarways Cl
Highlands
Woodland Dr
Wrecclesham
THE STREET
Westfield La
Cem
Chartwell
Rural
Shortheath Crest
Ltl Thurbans Cl
Gorse Cl
Gorse La
Ford Lane
Twyford La
Burnt Hill Rd
Shortheath
Cokenor Wd
Copse Way
Kings La
Pottery Lane
Broadwell Rd
Hth Cl
Quennells Hl
Greystead Pk
Woodcut Rd
Sunnydell La
Longhope Dr
Bat And Ball La
Wicket Hill
Birdhaven
Sandrock Hill
Bourne Dene
Bourne La
Upr Bourne La
ECHO BARN LANE
The Chine
Hollis Wood Dr
WRECCLESHAM HILL
Works
Wrecclesham Hill
65
B3384
Laurel Gv
Bower Rd
Beacon Cl
Rock Lane
Bndstn Cl
Burnt Hill Way
Jubilee La
Vine Wy
Broad Ha'penny
Thorn Rd
Browns Wk
Bridge Rd
Manley
Lavender La
Vine Cl
Surgery
Birch Cl
Appletands Cl
Gardener's Hill Road
Bound
White Post Lane
Glynswood
Clifton Close
Swiss Road
Swiss Cl
Boundstone Rd
Shrubbs La
Works
Rosemary La
High Street
The Copse
Clare Mead
GU10
Frensham Ct
The Avenue
Switchback La
Fullers Road
School Rd
Forest Glade
Bell Lane
Chapel Rd
Mayfield
Meadow Way
Orch End
Rowledge
Recreation Rd
Rowledge CE (Controlled) Prim School
PO
Cherry Tree Rd
Hadleys
Prospect Rd
Road
Church La
Pear Tree La
The Long Road
Hawthorn Lane
Fernbrae Cl
Frensham Road
Frensham Heights
Frensham Heights
A
B
C
D
59
68
482
83
45
44
143
1
2
3
4
5
1 grid square represents 500 metres

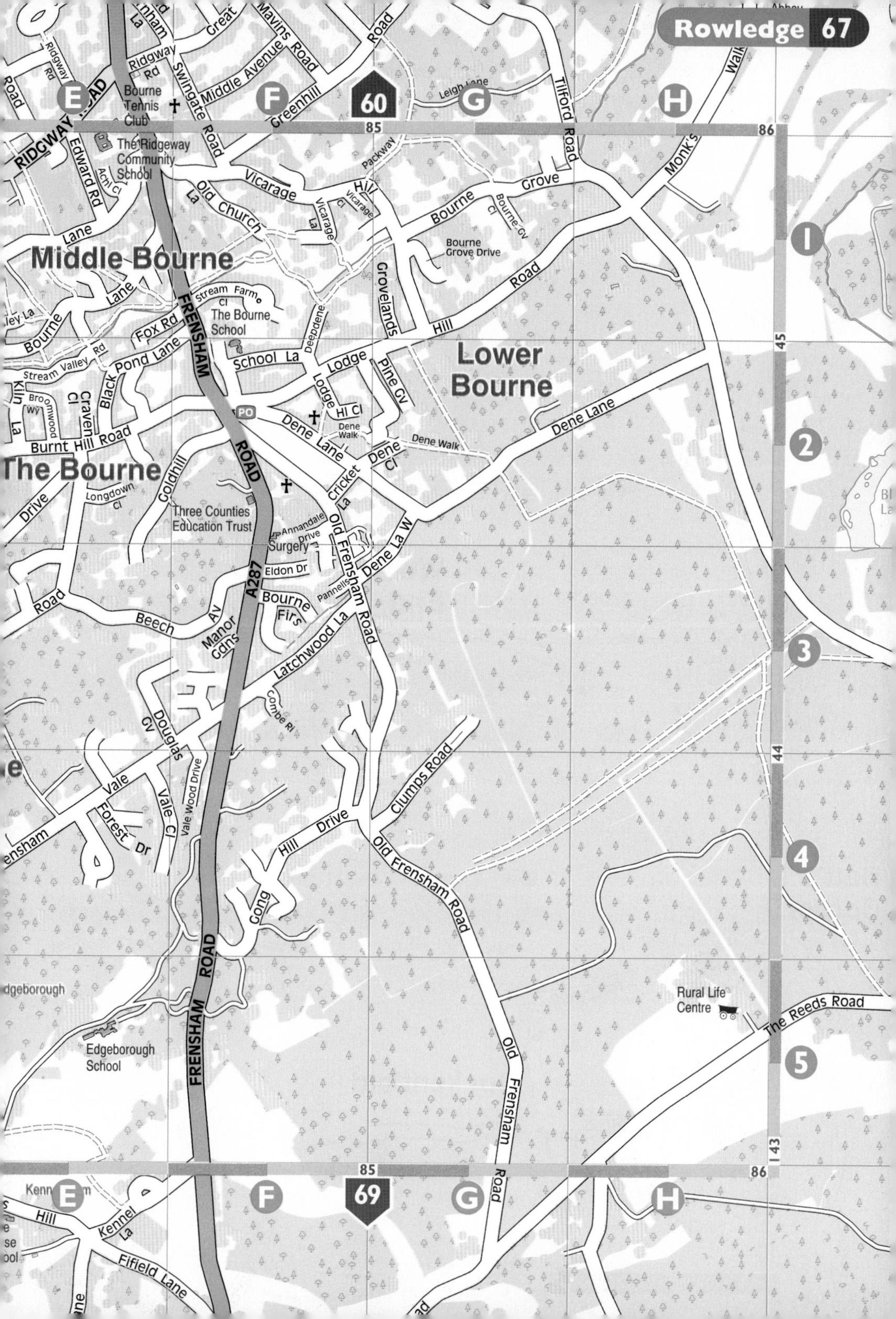
Middle Bourne
Lower Bourne
The Bourne
Ridgway Rd
Ridgway Road
Bourne Tennis Club
Swingate Road
Middle Avenue
Great Mavins Road
Greenhill Road
Leigh Lane
Tilford Road
Monk's Walk
The Ridgeway Community School
Edward Rd
Achi Cl
Old Church La
Vicarage Hill
Vicarage La
Vicarage Cl
Packway
Bourne Grove
Bourne Cl
Bourne Gv
Bourne Grove Drive
Lane
Bourne Lane
Stream Farm Cl
The Bourne School
Fox Rd
Stream Valley Rd
Black Pond Lane
School La
Deepdene
Grovelands
Hill Road
Lodge Hill
Lodge Hl Cl
Pine Gv
Dene Lane
Dene Walk
Dene Cl
Kiln La
Broomwood Wy
Craven Cl
Burnt Hill Road
Frensham Road
A287
PO
Coldhill
Longdown Cl
Drive
Three Counties Education Trust
Annandale Drive
Surgery
Cricket La
Old Frensham Road
Dene La W
Eldon Dr
Pannells
Road
Beech Av
Manor Gdns
Bourne Firs
Latchwood La
Combe Rl
Douglas Gv
Vale Wood Drive
Vale Cl
Vale
Forest Dr
Frensham
Clumps Road
Hill Drive
Gong
Edgeborough
Edgeborough School
Rural Life Centre
The Reeds Road
Kennel La
Hill
Fifield Lane
E F G H
1 2 3 4 5
60
69
85 86
45 44 143

Rowledge CE (Controlled) Prim School
Recreation Rd
PO
Cherry Tree Rd
Hadleys
Prospect Road
Church La
Hawthorn Lane
The Long Rd
Pear Tree La
Orch End
Way
66
Fernbrae Cl
482
83
43
Lickfolds
Boundary Road
Frensham Road
Heights
Frensham Heights School
Frensham Heights
Summerfield Lane
Broomfield La
Broomfield Lane
Broomfields
Short Comm
West End Lane
West End
Spreakley
Woodhill
42
Boundary Road
Batt's Corner
Pitt Farm
Mill
41
Bealeswood Lane
Boundary Road
Lake Lane
Dockenfield
Pitt Lane
Green La
The Street
Street
enfield
Lane
County
shire County
A
B
C
D
1
2
3
4
5
1 grid square represents 500 metres

Edgeborough School
Kennel Farm
Hill
Kennel La
Fifield Lane
Hamlash Lane
Sandy Lane
PO
Shortfield Road
The Reeds Road
Old Frensham Road
Millbridge
Pierreponte School
River Wey (South Branch)
Priory Lane
A287
The Street
Lovers La
Peakfield
St Marys CE Aided Infant School
Lane End
ham
Frensham Little Pond
Frensham Common Country Park
Lowicks House
Frensham Great Pond
Bacon
67
E
F
G
H
85
86
43
42
141
1
2
3
4
5

USING THE STREET INDEX

Street names are listed alphabetically. Each street name is followed by its postal town or area locality, the Postcode District, the page number, and the reference to the square in which the name is found.

Standard index entries are shown as follows:

Abbetts La *CBLY* GU15 ... **21** F3

Street names and selected addresses not shown on the map due to scale restrictions are shown in the index with an asterisk:

Abbeywood *ASHV* GU12 * ... **49** F3

GENERAL ABBREVIATIONS

ACC ... ACCESS
ALY ... ALLEY
AP ... APPROACH
AR ... ARCADE
ASS ... ASSOCIATION
AV ... AVENUE
BCH ... BEACH
BLDS ... BUILDINGS
BND ... BEND
BNK ... BANK
BR ... BRIDGE
BRK ... BROOK
BTM ... BOTTOM
BUS ... BUSINESS
BVD ... BOULEVARD
BY ... BYPASS
CATH ... CATHEDRAL
CEM ... CEMETERY
CEN ... CENTRE
CFT ... CROFT
CH ... CHURCH
CHA ... CHASE
CHYD ... CHURCHYARD
CIR ... CIRCLE
CIRC ... CIRCUS
CL ... CLOSE
CLFS ... CLIFFS
CMP ... CAMP
CNR ... CORNER
CO ... COUNTY
COLL ... COLLEGE
COM ... COMMON
COMM ... COMMISSION
CON ... CONVENT
COT ... COTTAGE
COTS ... COTTAGES
CP ... CAPE
CPS ... COPSE
CR ... CREEK
CREM ... CREMATORIUM
CRS ... CRESCENT
CSWY ... CAUSEWAY
CT ... COURT
CTRL ... CENTRAL
CTS ... COURTS
CTYD ... COURTYARD
CUTT ... CUTTINGS
CV ... COVE
CYN ... CANYON
DEPT ... DEPARTMENT
DL ... DALE
DM ... DAM
DR ... DRIVE
DRO ... DROVE
DRY ... DRIVEWAY
DWGS ... DWELLINGS
E ... EAST
EMB ... EMBANKMENT
EMBY ... EMBASSY
ESP ... ESPLANADE
EST ... ESTATE
EX ... EXCHANGE
EXPY ... EXPRESSWAY
EXT ... EXTENSION
F/O ... FLYOVER
FC ... FOOTBALL CLUB
FK ... FORK
FLD ... FIELD
FLDS ... FIELDS
FLS ... FALLS
FM ... FARM
FT ... FORT
FTS ... FLATS
FWY ... FREEWAY
FY ... FERRY
GA ... GATE
GAL ... GALLERY
GDN ... GARDEN
GDNS ... GARDENS
GLD ... GLADE
GLN ... GLEN
GN ... GREEN
GND ... GROUND
GRA ... GRANGE
GRG ... GARAGE
GT ... GREAT
GTWY ... GATEWAY
GV ... GROVE
HGR ... HIGHER
HL ... HILL
HLS ... HILLS
HO ... HOUSE
HOL ... HOLLOW
HOSP ... HOSPITAL
HRB ... HARBOUR
HTH ... HEATH
HTS ... HEIGHTS
HVN ... HAVEN
HWY ... HIGHWAY
IMP ... IMPERIAL
IN ... INLET
IND EST ... INDUSTRIAL ESTATE
INF ... INFIRMARY
INFO ... INFORMATION
INT ... INTERCHANGE
IS ... ISLAND
JCT ... JUNCTION
JTY ... JETTY
KG ... KING
KNL ... KNOLL
L ... LAKE
LA ... LANE
LDG ... LODGE
LGT ... LIGHT
LK ... LOCK
LKS ... LAKES
LNDG ... LANDING
LTL ... LITTLE
LWR ... LOWER
MAG ... MAGISTRATES'
MAN ... MANSIONS
MD ... MEAD
MDW ... MEADOWS
MEM ... MEMORIAL
MI ... MILL
MKT ... MARKET
MKTS ... MARKETS
ML ... MALL
MNR ... MANOR
MS ... MEWS
MSN ... MISSION
MT ... MOUNT
MTN ... MOUNTAIN
MTS ... MOUNTAINS
MUS ... MUSEUM
MWY ... MOTORWAY
N ... NORTH
NE ... NORTH EAST
NW ... NORTH WEST
O/P ... OVERPASS
OFF ... OFFICE
ORCH ... ORCHARD
OV ... OVAL
PAL ... PALACE
PAS ... PASSAGE
PAV ... PAVILION
PDE ... PARADE
PH ... PUBLIC HOUSE
PK ... PARK
PKWY ... PARKWAY
PL ... PLACE
PLN ... PLAIN
PLNS ... PLAINS
PLZ ... PLAZA
POL ... POLICE STATION
PR ... PRINCE
PREC ... PRECINCT
PREP ... PREPARATORY
PRIM ... PRIMARY
PROM ... PROMENADE
PRS ... PRINCESS
PRT ... PORT
PT ... POINT
PTH ... PATH
PZ ... PIAZZA
QD ... QUADRANT
QU ... QUEEN
QY ... QUAY
R ... RI
RBT ... ROUNDAB
RD ... RO
RDG ... RI
REP ... REPUB
RES ... RESERV
RFC ... RUGBY FOOTBALL C
RI ... R
RP ... RA
RW ... R
S ... SOU
SCH ... SCH
SE ... SOUTH E
SER ... SERVICE A
SH ... SH
SHOP ... SHOPP
SKWY ... SKYW
SMT ... SUM
SOC ... SOC
SP ... SP
SPR ... SPR
SQ ... SQU
ST ... STR
STN ... STAT
STR ... STRE
STRD ... STRA
SW ... SOUTH W
TDG ... TRAD
TER ... TERR
THWY ... THROUGH
TNL ... TUN
TOLL ... TOLL
TPK ... TURN
TR ... TR
TRL ... T
TWR ... TOW
U/P ... UNDERP
UNI ... UNIVER
UPR ... UP
V ... V
VA ... VA
VIAD ... VIAD
VIL ... V
VIS ... V
VLG ... VILL
VLS ... VI
VW ... V
W ... W
WD ... W
WHF ... WH
WK ... W
WKS ... WA
WLS ... W
WY ...
YD ... Y
YHA ... YOUTH HO

POSTCODE TOWNS AND AREA ABBREVIATIONS

ALDT ... Aldershot
ALTN ... Alton
ASC ... Ascot
ASHV ... Ash Vale
BAGS ... Bagshot
BFOR ... Bracknell Forest/Windlesham
BLKW ... Blackwater
BRAK ... Bracknell
CBLY ... Camberley
CHOB/PIR ... Chobham/Pirbright
CWTH ... Crowthorne
EWKG ... Wokingham east
FARN ... Farnborough
FLEETN ... Fleet north
FLEETS ... Fleet south
FNM ... Farnham
FRIM ... Frimley
HTWY ... Hartley Wintney
LTWR ... Lightwater
MFD/CHID ... Milford/Chiddingfold
RFNM ... Rural Farnham
RGUW ... Rural Guildford
SHST ... Sandh
WOKN/KNAP ... Woking north/Kna
WOKS/MYFD ... Woking south/May
YTLY ... Ya

A

B

C

D